Conures as Pets

Conure Facts & Information

Conure Bird Health, Where To Buy, Diet, Lifespan, Breeding, Fun Facts, Care, Habitat, And Much More!

By Lolly Brown

Foreword

Conures have been kept as pets for hundreds of years and was even mentioned in various works of literature dating back to the 18th century!

Conure parrots were admired by bird enthusiasts because of their amusing personalities and undeniable energy. Many conure pet owners believe that these birds are packed with a larger-than-life attitude wrapped in a small package!

Although Conures are truly a convenient choice as pets, these birds doesn't come with a thin instruction manual. Fear not! In this book you'll be easily guided on understanding your Conure, their nature, their behavior and characteristics, how you should feed and care for them and a whole lot more.

Embark on a wonderful journey of sharing your life with a Conure Parrot. Learn to maximize the great privilege of living with one and be able to share this unique and unforgettable experience just like your ancestors that came before you!

Table of Contents

Chapter One: Introduction

Conures have a reputation for having a knack of humor and being the noisiest bird among all the parrot species. Its reverberating loudness and spunky attitude are what keep these birds unique throughout the ages!

Aside from its attractive and variant colors, these birds also have an outgoing personality and they are very inquisitive in nature. They are very fond of performing tricks, so don't be surprise if your conure plays a trick on you!

They are recognized in eight distinct genera; these are *Aratinga, Nandayus, Ognorhynchus, Leptosittaca, Conuropsis, Cyanoliseus, Enicognathus and Pyrrhura* with more than 40 subspecies! Later on in this book, you will learn more about the different types of conure parrots so that you can choose what is best for you!

Conures are great as pets, though sometimes some people may find its loud nature unacceptable and its attitude is at times intimidating, but that's of course, part of who they are. They are clever and can be easily trained to perform tricks and mimic sounds like any other birds, although, conures are generally easy to care for because of its small size, you will still need some useful tips, so that you can maximize its true potential.

Conure parrots are definitely long-term companions. These birds have an average lifespan of more than 20 years! If you do it right, they will certainly live longer than you might expect. They're friendly but witty companions, and because of that you need some guidance on how to take care of them, raise them and possibly learn how to be like them as well as teach them to be like you!!

Fortunately, this ultimate guide will teach you on how to be the best Conure owner you can be! Inside this book, you will find tons of helpful information about Conure Parrots: how they live, how to deal with them and realize the great benefits of owning one!

Glossary of Important Terms

Archaeological – a scientific study of material remains (such as fossil relics and artifacts of human or animal species)

Avian – Pertaining to birds.

Asymptomatic – having or showing no symptoms of disease

Beak – The mouth of a bird consisting of the upper and lower mandibles.

Breast – The chest of a bird located between the chin and the abdomen.

Breeding – an act of producing young animals

Brood – a group of young birds all born at the same time.
Ceres – a waxy, fleshy covering at the base of the upper beak of birds

Chick – A newly hatched bird; a baby bird.

Clutch – The eggs laid by a female bird in a single setting.

Cuttlebone – the shell of a cuttlefish that is used for supplying cage birds with lime and salts.

Flock – A group of birds.

Fossils – reserved from a past geologic age

Hatching – The process through which baby birds emerge from the egg.

Hybrid – a conure that is produced by combining two different kinds of species.

Incubation – The act or process of keeping eggs warm which causes it to eventually hatch.

Nares – the openings of the bird's nose or nasal cavity.

Nape – back of the neck

Pinfeathers – a not fully developed feather emerging from the skin

Plumage – the feathers that cover the body of the bird

Sexual Dimorphism – Referring to physical differences between the sexes of the same species.

Suppler – ability to bent or twist easily

Stargazing – a twisted back in birds.

Taxonomy – The classification of species into order, family, genera, etc.

Tetra-Chromic – four color light vision including ultraviolet.

Urates – a salt of uric acid.

UVA – a radiation that causes tanning of the skin.

UVB – a radiation that is responsible for sunburn in the skin.

Wingspan – distance from the tip of one wing of a bird to the tip of the other wing.

Chapter Two: Meet Conures

The great thing about Conures is that they have huge personalities wrapped in a small package! They are very enchanting birds to care for and very low maintenance at the same time. Conures are very ideal pets especially for first time bird owners. But before getting a fascinating parrot as your pet, it's very important that you know what it is inside out! Like many other things, you need to have proper knowledge and invest a significant amount of time to truly study and understand where these birds are coming from. That is how you will determine if this kind of pet is the right choice, so that you know what you are dealing with.

On the next sections, you'll be introduced to the friendliest and one of the most energetic parrots in the world. Prepare to meet conures!

1.) *What are Conures?*

Conures, which are scientifically under the Subfamily of *Arinae*, are birds that are native to Latin America, Central and South America, Mexico and even in the Caribbean. These birds life expectancy is about 20 – 40 years!

They are relatively small parrots with a funny sociable attitude towards people, which makes them an interesting choice as pets.

These parrots had been popular since the 18th century especially in Latin America and Southern Chile.

Mostly conures are small in size but there are also medium- sized species. They have fluffy colorful feathers that also come in an array of different colors like red, lavish green, orange, white, vibrant yellow, and brown. Different variations of hybrid conures also exist, mainly for pet trade

Conures parrots have about 45 subspecies, classified into 8 types or genera; these are *Aratinga, Nandayus, Ognorhynchus, Leptosittaca, Conuropsis, Cyanoliseus, Enicognathus and Pyrrhura.*

Even if these birds are miniature, they have a reputation of being the loudest and love to screech big time, but the advantage of this is that they can be quickly taught to speak and perform cool tricks.

Aside from screaming, they are also fond of chewing and playing interesting games to keep them from being bored and also to satisfy their curious minds. They are totally witty and have a knack for a fun time!

Most Conures are generally easy to train and can be well-behaved as long as you provide them with adequate attention, interaction, and love. They can easily become part of the family and a loving companion if you are willing to put in the time and effort to take care of them.

2.) *Facts About Conures*

Conures can be easily identified because they have slender bodies, flared tails with narrow tips and heavy or light-colored beaks with broad ceres and super-fluffy feathers which make them really look cuddly and cute.

Their average size including tails is about 9 – 19 inches, with a wingspan of about 6 – 162 cm, and weighs about 73 – 190 grams. It has an average lifespan of 20 – 40 years.

In terms of their behavior and personality, they are quite notorious for having sharp screeching noise and bold attitude in everything. They will destroy and chew on any objects available, requires lots of interaction and at times nippy to unfamiliar faces. But they are primarily easy to tame and very friendly once they get to know you.

These parrots are omnivorous and usually feed on seeds, insects, fruit and nuts. Conures are not sexually dimorphic; the gender can only be determined through DNA sexing, they are also monogamous when choosing mates.

In terms of reproduction, conures reach their sexual maturity as early as 2 years old and breeding period usually occurs during spring; females' clutch size ranges from an average of 2 – 5 eggs and incubation lasts for about 23 – 27 days.

Just like any parrots, conures can be trained to mimic human speech and imitate other sounds by using their bifurcated trachea, which are equivalent to vocal cords in humans.

Quick Facts

- **Taxonomy**: phylum *Chordata*, class *Aves*, order *Psittaciformes*, family *Psittacidae*, Subfamily *Arinae*, Tribe *Arini*.
- **Distribution**: Latin America, South and Central America, Caribbean
- **Habitat**: Tropical dry forests, dry savannahs
- **Lifestyle**: Flock Oriented
- **Anatomical Adaptations**:
- **Breeding Season**: All year round; spring
- **Eggs**: 2 – 5 eggs
- **Incubation Period**: 23 – 27 days
- **Sexual Maturity** : 2 – 3 years old
- **Average Size**: 22 cm – 48 cm (9 – 19 in)
- **Average Weight**: 73 – 190 grams
- **Wingspan**: 6 – 162 cm (2 – 23 in)
- **Coloration**: red, green, orange, white, yellow, and brown
- **Sexual Dimorphism**: Sexually dimorphic
- **Diet**: Seeds, Insects, Fruit, Nuts (Omnivore)
- **Sounds**: Vocal Communicator
- **Interaction**: Highly Social
- **Lifespan**: 20 – 40 years

3.) *Conures in History*

There had been different citations of conures in literature particularly during the 18th century at around 1724. Father Jean B. Labat, a priest and missionary from France, once described a bird from the island of Guadeloupe called *Aratinga labati*, in which most people believed that he kept this bird as a pet.

Conures already existed for hundreds of years in Latin America particularly in Mexico and Chile.

In the 1800's conures were imported to Europe and United States where they were kept as pets by royalties and wealthy people.

During the 20th century especially during the 1900s, conures were already prominent in the United States and in several European countries. However, due to the two World Wars and bird diseases outbreaks, the number of parrot species decline.

In the 1960's, the Sun Conure was among the parrot species that were popularly bred and produced in captivity.

Today, bird importation is still restricted but many conure species are successfully bred in captivity and readily available in local pet stores and avian breeders.

4.) Types of Conures

Conures are small birds that came from a big parrot family. There are about 45 existing species of conures belonging to 8 main types or genera.

In this section, you will learn all of the different kinds of conures, their major characteristics, their colors as well as a recommended list of the most popular conures that are readily available and ideal as pets. There are lots to choose from and it'll be a just a quick and easy read of these marvelous species. Read on!

Here is a quick overview of the 8 genera with over 45 species of Conures.

4.1.) Genus *Aratinga*

Common Name	Scientific Name
• Sharp-tailed Conure	Aratinga acuticaudata
• Golden Conure	Aratinga guarouba
• Green Conure	Aratinga holochlora
• Red-throated Conure	Aratinga rubritorquis
• Finsch's Conure	Aratinga finschii
• Red-fronted Conure	Aratinga wagleri
• Hocking's Conure	Aratinga hockingi
• Chapman's Conure	Aratinga alticola
• Mitred Conure	Aratinga mitrata
• Red-masked Conure	Aratinga erythrogenys
• White-eyed Conure	Aratinga leucophthalma
• Hispaniolan Conure	Aratinga chloroptera
• Cuban Conure	Aratinga euops
• Golden-capped Conure	Aratinga auricapilla
• Jandaya Conure	Aratinga jandaya
• Sun Conure	Aratinga solstitialis
• Sulfur-breasted Conure	Aratinga pintoi
• Dusky-headed Conure	Aratinga weddellii
• Jamaican Conure	Aratinga nana

• Orange-fronted Conure	<u>Aratinga canicularis</u>
• Cactus Conure	<u>Aratinga cactorum</u>
• St. Thomas Conure	<u>Aratinga pertinax</u>
• Peach-fronted Conure	<u>Aratinga aurea</u>

4.2.) Genus *Nandayus*

Common Name	Scientific Name
• Nanday Conure	<u>Nandayus nenday</u>

4.3) Genus *Ognorhynchus*

Common Name	Scientific Name
• Yellow-eared Conure	<u>Ognorhynchus icterotis</u>

4.4) Genus *Leptosittaca*

Common Name	Scientific Name
• Golden-plumed Conure	<u>Leptosittaca branickii</u>

4.5) Genus *Conuropsis*

Common Name	Scientific Name
• Carolina Conure	<u>Conuropsis carolinensis</u>

4.6) Genus *Cyanoliseus*

Common Name	Scientific Name
• Patagonian Conure	Cyanoliseus patagonus

4.7) Genus *Enicognathu*

Common Name	Scientific Name
• Austral Conure	Enicognathus ferrugineus
• Slender-billed Conure	Enicognathus leptorhynchus

4.8) Genus *Pyrrhura*

Common Name	Scientific Name
• Blue-throated Conure	Pyrrhura cruentata
• Maroon-bellied Conure	Pyrrhura frontalis
• Crimson-belied Conure	Pyrrhura perlata
• Green-cheeked Conure	Pyrrhura molinae
• White-eared Conure	Pyrrhura leucotis
• Painted Conure	Pyrrhura picta
• Demerara Conure	Pyrrhura egregia
• Santa Marta Conure	Pyrrhura viridicata
• El Oro Conure	Pyrrhura orcesi
• Maroon-tailed Conure	Pyrrhura melanura

• Black-capped Conure	Pyrrhura rupicola
• White-necked Conure	Pyrrhura albipectus
• Red-eared Conure	Pyrrhura hoematotis
• Brown-breasted Conure	Pyrrhura calliptera
• Rose-crowned Conure	Pyrrhura rhodocephala

Below is a quick comprehensive overview of the different types of conure species sorted by genera. Quick facts and descriptions are also provided. Later on in this book, you'll be given a list of the most popular conures which are ideal as pets.

Genus Aratinga

The Aratinga genus has the most number of conure species among the conure genera; it is composed of 25 species, with approximately 20 subspecies. Aratinga Conures are native to Central and South America, particularly in Mexico and Argentina. The environmental condition of these species varies from tropical rainforests to savannahs, deserts to semi- deserts, and from mountains to sea level.

Popular conure species like the Sun Conure, Jenday Conure. Peach-fronted Conure, Red-masked Conure, and Mitred Conure all belong to Genus Aratinga.

Sharp-tailed Conure

Length: 34 (13.5 in)

Wingspan: 166 - 207 mm (6.5 in - 8 in)

Distribution: Brazil, Bolivia, Venezuela

Subspecies:

Blue-crowned Conure

Bolivian Blue-crowned Conure

Venezuelan Blue-crowned Conure

Margarita Conure

Golden Conure

Length: 34 cm (13.5 in)

Distribution: Northeast Brazil

Description: The plumage is yellow, with greenish flight-feathers and bluish-horned colored beak

Green Conure

Length: 32 – 34 cm (12.5 in - 13.5 in)

Wingspan: 160 mm - 185 mm (6.25 in -7.25 in)

Distribution: Mexico

Subspecies:

Brewster's Green Conure

Nicaraguan Green Conure

Socorro Green Conure

Red-throated Conure

Length: 30 cm (12 in)

Wingspan: 152-163 mm (6 in - 6.5 in)

Distribution: Guatemala, Nicaragua

Description: Its plumage is color green with yellowish-green abdomen and under-wings

Finsch's Conure

Length: 28 cm (11 in)

Distribution: Nicaragua, Panama

Description: It has yellowish-green abdomen with red fore crown and under wings and horn-colored beak

Red-fronted Conure

Length: 34 cm - 40 cm (13.5 in - 15.5 in)

Distribution: Colombia, Venezuela, Ecuador, Peru

Subspecies:

Peter's Conure

Scarlet-fronted Conure

Carriker's Conure

Hocking's Conure

Length: 38 cm (15 in)

Distribution: Peru

Description: It has green plumage with dark red-color around the eyes and olive-yellowish tail feathers

Chapman's Conure

Length: 36 cm (14 in)

Distribution: Peru, Bolivia

Description: Its plumage is greenish-blue with scattered red feathers around the eyes and blackish legs.

Mitred Conure

Length: 37 cm (14.5 in) - 38 cm (15 in)

Distribution: Peru, Argentina

Subspecies:

Northern Mitred Conure

Tucumán Mitred Conure

Red-masked Conure

Length: 33 cm (13 in)

Distribution: Western Ecuador, Northwest Peru

Description: Mostly green in color with yellowish tail feathers and red thighs and under wings

White-eyed Conure

Length: 32 cm (12.5 in) - 34 cm (13.5 in)

Wingspan: 170 mm - 195 mm

Distribution: French Guiana, Colombia, Brazil, Peru, Ecuador

Subspecies:

White-eyed Conure

Ecuadorian White-eyed Conure

Argentinian White-eyed Conure

Hispaniolan Conure

Length: 32 cm (12.5 in)

Distribution: Puerto Rico

Subspecies:

Hispaniolan Conure

Puerto Rican Conure also known as Mauge's Conure

Cuban Conure

Length: 26 cm (10 in)

Distribution: Cuba

Description: Its head, nape and breast typically has scattered red feathers with greyish- brown feet

Golden-capped Conure

Length: 30 cm (12 in)

Distribution: Brazil

Subspecies:

Golden-fronted Conure

Jandaya Conure

Length: 30 cm (12 in)

Distribution: Brazil

Description: Its plumage is green with red-colored forehead and a mixture of red and orange under wing-coverts as well as black-colored beak.

Sun Conure

Length: 30 cm (12 in)
Distribution: Northeast Brazil
Description: It has a black-colored flight feathers and beak with yellow plumage and a combination of yellow and orange under-wings and under-tails.

Sulfur-breasted Conure

Length: 30 cm (12 in)
Distribution: Brazil
Description: Its plumage is yellow with an orange-tinge in the forehead, abdomen, and lower back and blackish beak grey-colored feet.

Dusky-headed Conure

Length: 28 cm (11 in)
Distribution: Colombia, Ecuador, Peru, Brazil
Description: It has a green-colored body with a greyish-brown head and greyish-red cere.

Jamaican Conure

Length: 24 cm (9.5 in) - 26 cm (10 in)

Distribution: Jamaica

Subspecies:

Aztec Conure also known as Olive-throated Conure

Eastern Aztec Conure

Orange-fronted Conure

Length: 24 cm (9.5 in)

Distribution: Mexico, Costa Rica

Subspecies:

Eastern Mexican Petz's Conure

Western Mexican Petz's Conure

Cactus Conure

Length: 25 cm (10 in)

Distribution: Brazil

Subspecies:

Pale Cactus Conure

St. Thomas Conure

Length: 24 -25 cm (10 in)

Distribution: Virgin Islands, Brazil, Venezuela, Colombia, French Guiana

Subspecies:

Bonaire Brown-throated Conure

Brown-throated Conure

Sinú Brown-throated Conure

Aruba Brown-throated Conure

Colombian Brown-throated Conure

Tortuga Brown-throated Conure

Margarita Brown-throated Conure

Venezuelan Brown-throated Conure

Guyana Brown-throated Conure

Surinam Brown-throated Conure

Brazilian Brown-throated Conure

Tapajós Brown-throated Conure

Brown-eared Conure

Peach-fronted Conure

Length: 26 cm (10 in) - 30 cm (12 in)

Wingspan 133 - 152 mm (5 - 6 in)

Distribution: Bolivia, Argentina

Subspecies:

Greater Golden-crowned Conure

Genus Nandayus

The Nanday Conure, which is scientifically known as, *Nandayus nenday* is the only known species in the Nandayus genus.

It is also known to have different common names such as the Black-masked Conure, Nanday Parakeet, and Black-hooded Conure. This specie is typically found in northern Argentina, Paraguay, and southeastern Bolivia particularly in Mato Grosso. It also inhabits parts of Northern America, and some of its colonies are found in southern and eastern parts of the United States.

Nanday Conure

Length: 30 cm (12 in)

Distribution: Brazil, Bolivia, Paraguay, Argentina

Description: Its head and beak is black with the underside tail is greenish with blue tips.

Genus Ognorhynchus

The Yellow-eared Conure or Yellow-eared Parrot which is scientifically known as *Ognorhynchus icterotis* is the only known species under Genus Ognorhynchus. It is an endangered species native to western Colombia.

Yellow-eared Conure

Length: 42 cm (16.5 in)

Distribution: Colombia, Ecuador

Description: It has a yellow ear-coverts; with yellowish wings and black beak

Genus Leptosittaca

The Golden-plumed Conure or Golden-plumed Parrot, which is scientifically known as *Leptosittaca branickii* is the only known specie under the Leptosittaca genus. It is native and has a large distribution in several parts of Colombia. However, due to habitat destruction and bird smuggling their numbers are declining and may soon be critically endangered.

Golden-plumed Conure

Length: 26 cm (10 in)

Distribution: Colombia, Peru

Description: Its forehead is brownish – orange with yellowish-green ear-coverts and feathers.

Genus Conuropsis

The Carolina Conure, which is scientifically known as *Conuropsis carolinensis* is the only known species under Genus Conuropsis. This specie is native to eastern United States particularly in Ohio Valley that reaches to the Gulf of Mexico. Unfortunately, this specie was already extinct since 1918 due to a number of reasons such deforestation and bird trading. It had a green-colored plumage with yellow head and scattered reddish feathers on its beak.

Carolina Conure

Length: 30 cm (12 in)

Distribution: Southeast United States.

Subspecies:

Louisiana Parakeet

Genus Cyanoliseus

The Patagonian Conure or Burrowing Parrot, which is scientifically known as *Cyanoliseus patagonus* is very common in Argentina and Chile, with a migration distribution found in Uruguay during the winter.

Patagonian Conure

Length: 45 cm (18 in)

Wingspan: 232 mm - 252 mm (9 in - 10 in)

Distribution: Argentina, Uruguay

Subspecies:

Andean Patagonian Conure

Greater Patagonian Conure

Genus Enicognathu

The Enicognathus genus is composed of two species, with only one known subspecies; these species are called the Austral Conure and Slender-bill Conure. These birds are native in southern Argentina and Chile. They typically live in farmlands and wooded areas.

Austral Conure

Length: 34 cm (13.5 in)

Wingspan: 176 - 193 mm (6.9 in - 7.6 in)

Distribution: Southern Argentina, Chile

Subspecies:
Chilean Conure

Slender-billed Conure
Length: 40 cm (15.75 in)
Distribution: Central Chile
Description: It has a brownish to blackish edging all the way up to the head with reddish-brown tail and grey-colored feet.

Genus Pyrrhura

The last but definitely not the least is genus Pyrrhura. This genus is made up of 22 species with more than over 20 subspecies. They inhabit tropical and subtropical regions in Central America and South America as well as Panama and Costa Rica. This genus also includes some of the most popular conures such as the Painted Conure, the Green-cheeked Conure, Black-capped Conure, and Pearly Conure. Due to deforestation and illegal bird trading, some of these species are highly endangered.

Blue-throated Conure
Length: 30 cm (12 in)
Distribution: Brazil
Description: Its throat and upper breast is colore blue and has an olive-colored tail and flight feathers.

Maroon-bellied Conure

Length: 26 cm (10 in)

Distribution: Southeast Brazil, Paraguay, Bolivia

Subspecies:

Azara's Conure

Blaze-winged Conure

Pearly Conure

Length: 24 cm (9.5 in)

Distribution: Northern Brazil

Subspecies:

Crimson-bellied Conure

Pearly Conure

Miritiba Pearly Conure

Neumann's Pearly Conure

Green-cheeked Conure

Length: 26 cm (10 in)

Distribution: Highlands of Eastern Bolivia; Argentina, Brazil

Subspecies:

Argentina Conure

Crimson-tailed Conure

Sordid Conure (Yellow-sided Conure)

Santa Cruz Conure

White-eared Conure

Length: 22 cm (8.5 in)

Distribution: Brazil, Venezuela

Subspecies:

Brazilian Grey-breasted Conure

Pfrimer's Conure

Emma's Conure

Monagas White-eared Conure

Painted Conure

Length: 22 cm (8.5 in)

Wingspan: 115 mm - 130 mm (4.5 in - 5 in)

Distribution: Venezuela, Colombia

Subspecies:

Santarem Conure

Smaller Painted Conure

Prince Lucien's Conure

Rose-headed Conure

Jaraquiel Conure

Magdalena Conure

Pantchenko's Conure

Azuero Conure

Fiery-shouldered Conure

Length: 24 - 25 cm (10 in)

Distribution: Venezuela

Subspecies:

Gran Sabana Conure

Santa Marta Conure

Length: 25 cm (10 in)

Distribution: Colombia

Description: It has a narrow red band in its forehead, with a brownish-purple nape, throat and breast feathers and horn-colored beak.

El Oro Conure

Length: 22 cm (8.5 in)

Distribution: Ecuador

Description: Its forehead is red with a red tinge in the abdomen and dark-grey feet

Maroon-tailed Conure

Length: 24 cm (9.5 in)

Wingspan: 125 mm - 135 mm (4.92 in - 5.31 in)

Distribution: Peru, Brazil, Venezuela, Colombia

Subspecies:

Souancé's Conure

Berlepsch's Conure

Pacific Black-tailed Conure

Chapman's Conure

Black-capped Conure

Length: 25 cm (9.5 in)

Distribution: Peru, Brazil, Bolivia

Subspecies:

Sandia Conure

White-necked Conure

Length: 24 cm (9.5 in)

Distribution: Southeast Ecuador

Description: It has a narrow brownish-red frontal band with white-colored throat and nape and grey-colored beak.

Red-eared Conure

Length: 25 cm – 26 cm (10 in)

Distribution: Venezuela

Subspecies:

Cubiro Red-eared Conure

Brown-breasted Conure

Length: 22 cm (8.5 in)

Distribution: Central Colombia

Description: Its throat, upper breast, and sides of neck is a color combination of grey, brown and red, with greyish-brown feet

Rose-crowned Conure

Length: 24 cm (9.5 in)

Distribution: Venezuela

Description: Its forehead, crown, back of head, and nape is primarily red, with maroon-colored ear-coverts and horn-colored beak.

Hoffman's Conure

Length: 24 cm (9.5 in)

Distribution: Southern Costa Rica

Subspecies:

Chiriqui Conure

Ideal Conure Pets

Here is the list of some of the best conure species that are commonly available in the market and are ideal as pets. Check if their characteristics suit your own personality, so that you can choose the best option for you.

Sun Conure (*Aratinga solstitialis*)

Characteristics:

The Sun Conure is one of the most sought-after conure species because they are highly sociable and very sweet birds. It is extremely vocal and very alert at the same time. It is energetic, funny, and loves to perform tricks, which makes it a very playful pet. If you are as energetic as the sun conure then maybe this is the right one for you.

Jenday Conure (*Aratinga janday*)

Characteristics:

These species' personality is very similar to sun conure's. The flipside is there are times that they are very demanding and really seek human attention and interaction. They are also one of the noisiest types of conures, so take that into consideration especially if you live in an apartment. However, if you can tolerate their loudness, you'll surely enjoy their fun company, they will never bore you.

Blue Crowned Conure (*Thectocercus acuticaudata*)

Characteristics:

These birds are very intelligent, naturally sweet and love to play tricks as well. They are also very good at speaking, but they get bored easily, that's why you need to provide many destructive toys that they can chew and have fun with to satisfy their curious minds. Do you like to talk and communicate to people? Why not try acquiring a Blue-Crowned Conure, this might be the perfect pet for you!

Nanday Conure (*Nandayus nenday*)

Characteristics:

Nanday Conures also make excellent pets, but like many conure species they also tend to be very noisy and could destroy everything in your house if left unattended. They are clever birds and are also very easy to train.

Red Masked Conure (*Psittacara erythrogenys*)

Characteristics:

These birds are one of the larger types of conure species. They are also very playful and active birds that make good pets. Like the Blue-Crowned Conure they are also excellent talkers and also loves to interact with humans. Just decide on what color you prefer, red or blue?

Patagonian Conure (*Cyanoliseus patagonus*)

Characteristics:

The Patagonian Conures loves to cuddle and they are very affectionate. Their large size makes them the ideal choice for someone who is attracted to conures, but who would prefer a larger size bird as a pet. If you like a bird that is comfortable in nuzzling, then this one is for you!

Peach Fronted Conure (*Eupsittula aurea*)

Characteristics:

Not a talker? No problem, the Peach Fronted Conure is one of the rather quite birds in conure standards, which makes them very ideal as pets especially if you are living in apartments or if you enjoy silence! They are sweet, also playful but not loud. They are not aggressive and they pretty much like to just stay put, but they still need care and attention.

Dusky Headed Conure (*Eupsittula weddellii*)

Characteristics:

Another quite type of conure are a Dusky Headed Conures, they are not that attractive or striking like the other species but the great thing about them is that they are not as demanding unlike other birds. They are ideal for children and young at hearts.

Maroon Bellied Conure (*Pyrrhura frontalis*)

Characteristics:

Maroon Bellied Conures loves to interact to people however speaking is its major weakness. The good news is that they are intelligent birds which make them highly trainable. They are also screechers but not as loud as their other relative conures, so if you want a pet you can play with, and enjoy a balance of noise and silence, then this bird is the one you need!

Green Cheeked Conure (*Pyrrhura molinae*)

Characteristics:

Last but definitely not the least is Green-Cheeked Conures. They are also relatively quiet which makes them ideal if you are living in an apartment and is also suitable for people with sensitive hearing. They love to whistle instead of screech and also do well in communal aviaries. They are clever, loving and sociable birds and they are easy to introduce to other species. However, they are already endangered in the wild and probably a bit harder to acquire in local pet stores, so if you ever get to have one, consider yourself very lucky!

Chapter Three: Conures' Requirements

Are you now thinking of getting a Conure? No problem! After learning what Conures are, where they come from, how they live and its different types, it's time to give you practical tips on what you need to know before buying one.

In this chapter, you will get a whole lot of information on its pros and cons, its average monthly costs as well as the things you need so that you will be well on your way to becoming a legitimate Conure pet owner -should you decide to be one! It's up to you! Read on!

1.) *Pros and Cons of Conures*

The information listed below is the advantages and disadvantages of owning Conures:

Pros

- **Personality:** They are playful, lively and bold
- **Appearance:** Vibrant and vividly colorful with fluffy feathers
- **Abilities:** Known to perform awesome tricks and can also be taught to speak
- **Cost:** They are very cheap and low maintenance
- **Impact on Humans:** They are cuddly and loves to interact with people; great long-time companions.

Cons

- **Noise:** They are loud screamers and have ear-piercing screeches. Better be ready, they are noisiest parrot species in the world.
- **Damage to Your Home**: They love to chew up and destroy your wooden furniture if left out of the cage.
- **Behavior:** They can have mood swings and can be a bit nippy to strangers
- **Speaking Ability**: Not that good in speaking but can be trained

2.) *Conures Behavior with other pets*

There is actually no general rule when introducing your pet parrot with other types or species of birds, sometimes they'll get along, sometimes they won't.

Fortunately, conures in general are very welcoming to other species regardless of its kind! They are the friendliest among all parrots, and you as the owner don't have to worry if ever you would introduce them to other birds or pets, they love to hang out with everyone including people!

There is however a flipside, specifically to smaller conures because sometimes they get so aggressive that they tend to fearlessly tackle bigger parrots and they also like to mess with smaller birds like budgies or parrotlets by grabbing their feathers or nipping its toes, this of course could potentially start a violent relationship with one another. They are indeed, small but sometimes terrible birds so keep a tight watch over them especially if you just introduced them or if they interact with other species.

It is also best done if the conures are still young, because they are still vulnerable and can be very accepting of other members once they get used to it.

As a general rule, you can introduce other types of birds but do so with caution so that they could easily warm up with their new feathered friends.

Unlike other birds that are highly individual, Conures love to be in flocks when they're in the wild or even in captivity. It'll be easy to train them to like other parrots, though sometimes they can be a bit witty.

Experts also suggest that the best behaved conures are those who were exposed to lots of change in the environment and the ones who were trained to socialize with people, because they become more adjusted.

3.) Ease and Cost of Care

Owning a Conure parrot is very inexpensive and keeping one is also very low maintenance, since they are small birds. However, the supplies needed in keeping one will definitely add up to your daily life expenses, if you want to keep a conure as a pet you should be able to cover the necessary costs it entails.

In this section you will receive an overview of the expenses associated with purchasing and keeping a Conure as a pet.

a.) Initial Costs

The initial expenses associated with keeping Conures as pets include the cost of the bird itself as well as the cage, cage accessories, toys, and grooming supplies.

You will find an overview of these costs below as well as the estimated total expense for keeping a Macaw:

Purchase Price: starts at $175 - $1,000

As established earlier Conures are miniatures in size, which means that the price for purchasing one is quite cheaper compare to other birds. However, it also depends on the size of the bird, some conures are smaller which tends to be cheaper and some are medium-sized which could cost more. Also, hybrid conures with different colors could have more value.

The general rules in these birds are, the more colorful, rarer and clever it is, the more expensive it can be. So better check your budget to see which conures is best for you.

Cage: starts at $115 - $700

The bigger, the better! Even if Conures are small, it's a general rule for birds that they live in cages where they could have the luxury of space, after all that is where they're going to spend most of their time right? So pick the right cage for your conure, so that they'll enjoy life like you!

Accessories: more or less $100 in total

If you bought a cage, you'll definitely need cage accessories like perches, lights, feeding dishes, stands, cage covers and harnesses for your Conures. Accessories can be quite expensive depending on the brand as well as the quality and size of your purchase. Conures are quite naughty birds at times, they'll chew everything! Watch out!

Toys: more or less $50

Conures loves to chew things especially toys! They will easily destroy any toy that came there way, which usually means that you may need to keep buying more often. Like other parrots, they need plenty of stimulation to keep their intelligent and curious minds entertained. The price of the toys depends on the brand you choose to buy.

Keep birdie boredom at bay with chewable toys for your conure.

Grooming Supplies: more or less $50 in total

As part of pet hygiene, your feathered friend needs to be cleaned and properly groomed. There are lots of grooming supplies that you can buy online or in your local pet store. Again, the brand and quality of the product affect the price range to keep your conures clean and healthy.

Initial Cost for Conures	
Cost Type	**Approximate Cost**
Purchase Price	$175 (£131.85)
Cage	$115 (£86.64)
Accessories	$100 (£75.34)
Toys	$50 (£37.67)
Grooming Supplies	$50 (£37.67)
Total	$490(£369.17)

*Please note that these amounts are computed at the starting price and converted at the current exchange rate. Costs may vary.

b.) Monthly Costs

The monthly costs associated with keeping a Conure can be quite expensive even if they are generally low maintenance. Some of the things that needs to be bought on a monthly basis like food supplements, cleaning materials and even veterinary care every now and then will definitely add up to your expenses. Below are the estimate monthly costs it entails.

Bird Food (seeds, pellets, treats, fruits, vegetables, etc.): approximately $50 per month

Your conure needs a varied and healthy diet. There's a massive selection of high quality seed diets, complete food and pelleted foods to choose from both online and in your local pet stores, not to mention some treats you might want to buy especially when they're doing tricks! The cost will depend on the brand as well as the nutritional value of the food.

Feeding a variety of these foods, alongside fruits and vegetables is the key to a healthy parrot.

Cleaning Supplies: at least $10 per month

You don't need brand new cleaning supplies every month, but of course, you will run out of bird shampoo and soap eventually. Just include it in your budget.

Veterinary Care: starts at $150 - $1,000 or more

Conures rarely get sick compared to other types of parrots, but it's important to keep them healthy by taking them to an avian vet for medical check-up every now and then. Avian vets are trained specifically to work with exotic birds whereas a general practicing vet may not be familiar with their needs and treatments especially if they are sick, not to mention the medicines needed.

If in case, this happens it's better and wiser to set aside a portion of your budget for any medical needs that will come up.

Additional Costs: at least $10 per month

In addition to all of these monthly costs you should plan for occasional extra costs like repairs to your Conure cage, replacement toys, food supplements, medicines etc. You won't have to cover these costs every month but you should include it in your budget to be safe.

Here is the overview of your total monthly expenses for the needs of your pet Conure.

Monthly Costs for Conures	
Cost Type	**Approximate Cost**
Bird Food	$50 (£37.67)

Cleaning Supplies	$10 (£7.53)
Veterinary Care (optional)	$150 (£113.01)
Additional Costs	$10 (£7.53)
Total	$220 (£165.75)

*Please note that these amounts are computed at the starting price and converted at the current exchange rate. Costs may vary.

Chapter Four: Tips in Buying Conures

If you are still interested in reading this chapter, that only means one thing: you have already decided to buy a Conure. Good choice, they are really fun birds, you'll surely enjoy being with them!

Here you will learn tips and tricks on how to select a healthy conure, where to find the right breeder as well as the laws and permit you need to be aware of before buying.

1.) Restrictions and Regulations in United States

If you are planning to acquire a Conure as your pet, then you have to think beyond the cage. There are certain restrictions and regulations that you need to be aware of, because it will not only serve as protection for your bird but also for you. Here are some things you need to know regarding the acquirement of Conure both in United States and in Great Britain.

a.) What is CITES?

CITES stands for Convention on International Trade in Endangered Species of Wild Fauna and Flora. It protects Conures by regulating its import, export, and re-export through an international convention authorized through a licensing system.

It is also an international agreement, drafted by the International Union for Conservation of Nature (IUCN), which aims to ensure that the trade in specimens of wild animals and plants does not threaten their survival.

Different species are assigned in different appendix statuses such as Appendix I, II or III etc. These appendices indicate the level of threat to the current population of the bird with consideration to their likely ability to rebound in the wild with legal trade.

b.) Appendix I and II of CITES

Some birds are considered potentially endangered or highly threatened as indicated in CITES' Appendix I while some are not (Appendix II). In this section, you'll learn the differences between the two appendices and how to get the permits necessary.

Appendix I simply means that the birds included on this list are most likely endangered species and may require import or export permit to prevent illegal trading.

Most species of conures are listed on Appendix II, which means that they are not necessarily threatened with extinction but are still vulnerable in becoming endangered. International trade may be granted an export permit or certificate and no import permit is required for the species listed in Appendix II, although some countries make require such permits for safety purposes.

The Division of Management Authority processes applications for CITES permits for the United States. You should allow at least 60 days for the review of your permit applications.

For more information on how to apply for a CITES permit please visit their website at: <http://www.fws.gov/international/cites/>

2.) Permit in Great Britain and Australia

In Great Britain and Australia you may need a permit for you to be able to import, export, or travel with your Conure. This permit is called an **Animal Movement License**.

Aside from the CITES permit, sometimes a Pet Bird Import License and a veterinary health certificate are required before bringing your bird in Great Britain, the purpose of this is to prevent the spread of diseases if the bird is a carrier.

You can apply for a Pet Bird Import License through this link: <http://AHITchelmsford@animalhealth.gsi.gov.uk.>

Like in the United States being aware of the regulations and getting a license is an important thing you need to consider before you acquire, import or export a bird. This does not only protect the animals but it can also avoid confiscation of your pet.

3.) Practical Tips in Buying Conures

Now that you are already aware and have prior knowledge about the legal aspects of owning a conure, the next step is purchasing one through a local pet store or a legitimate breeder.

Here are some recommendations for finding a reputable conure parrot breeders in United States and in Great Britain.

a.) How to Find a Conure Breeder

The first thing you need to do is to look for a legit avian breeder or pet store in your area that specializes in Conures.

You can also find great avian breeders online but you have to take into consideration the validity of the breeder. It is highly recommended that you see your new bird in person before buying anything on the internet. You can find several recommended list of Conure local breeder websites later in this book.

If possible, spend as much time as you can with your prospective new Conure before buying it. Interact with the bird and see how it is with you.

Continue the diet of the bird as advised by the store owner or breeder to maintain its eating habits. Look for any health problems or issues as well.

Finally, only purchase a Conure that is banded. Banding means the bird have a small metal band on one of its legs placed at birth by the breeder which is inscribed with the bird's clutch number, date of birth and the breeder number.

Leg bands are indicators that the purchaser and the bird itself are in the country legally and have not been smuggled.

b.) Local Conure Breeders in the United States

Here are the lists of available Conure breeders in the United States sorted by each species with its current rate.

Availability and costs of these Conures may vary over time, please check the links provided for any updates.

Black-Capped Conure

Birdmans Baby Parrots

5668 N Lincoln Ave Chicago, Illinois

Website: www.birdmansparrots.com

Tel. No.: 773-317-3785

Price: $375.00

AJ'S Feathered Friends

804 N. La Fox Street. South Elgin, IL 60177

Website: www.ajspetshop.com

Tel. No.: 847-695-5624

Price: $400.00

Something Cheeky

Clayton, North Carolina 27520

Website: www.somethingcheeky.com

Tel. No.: 1-919-585-2241

Price: $350.00

In A Pickle Parrots

7924 Broadview Road, Broadview Heights, Ohio 44147

Website: www.inapickleparrots.com

Tel. No.: 440-627-6477

Email: Inapickleaviary@aol.com

Price: $325.00

World of Birds

15 Perry Street, Chester, New Jersey 07930

Website: www.worldofbirds.com

Tel. No.: 908-879-2291

Email: worldofbirds@optonline.net

Price: Not listed

Morning Glory Birds

West Hempstead, New York 11552

Website: www.facebook.com/glory.birds.7

Tel. No.: 516-972-3860

Price: $295.00

Featherheads

Port charlotte, Florida 33948

Website:http://www.birdbreeders.com/breeder/13627/feathe rheads-florida-port-charlotte-FL

Tel. No.: 813-679-4961

Price: $250.00

Blue-Crown Conures

Ginos Exiotic Birds

Blue Jay, CA 92317

Website: http://www.birdbreeders.com/bird/123210/scarlet-macaw

Tel. No.: 176-095-604-66

Email: Gmorrialle@gmail.com

Price: $1,000.00

Fancy Feathers

31 Roseland Avenue, Caldwell, New Jersey

Website: www.fancyfeathersaviary.com

Tel. No.: 973-403-2900

E-mail: ddargenio@gmail.com

Price: $700.00

The Bird Lady

17044 I-20, Lindale, Texas 75771

Website: http://www.birdbreeders.com/breeder/7816/the-bird-lady-east-of-dallas-off-of-i-20-TX/reviews

Tel. No.: 956-309-0750

E-mail: debinmcallen@att.net

Price: $750.00

SpringOak

Dripping Springs, Texas 78620

Website:http://www.birdbreeders.com/breeder/5561/springo

ak-dripping-springs-TX

Tel. No.: 512-630-1626

Email: sherylcoffman1@gmail.com

Price: $700.00

The Parrots Nest Of Maryland

4508 G Lower Beckleysville Road, Hampstead, Mary Land

Website: http://www.birdbreeders.com/bird/119312/blue-

crown-conure

Tel. No.: 410-374-1636

Email: livesaybrian@aol.com

Price: $700.00

Blue-Throat Conures

Birdmans Baby Parrots

5668 N Lincoln Ave Chicago, Illinois

Website: www.birdmansparrots.com

Tel. No.: 773-317-3785

Price: $250.00

Cherry-Head Conure

Linville's Aviary

Miami, Florida 33174

Website:http://www.birdbreeders.com/breeder/2920/linvilles
-aviary-miami-FL

Tel. No.: 305-968-1536

E-mail: cerbyu@aol.com

Price: $450.00

Crimson-Bellied Conures

Avian Events, LLC

Conyers, GA 30094

Website: www. avianevents.com

Tel. No.: 770-500-2882

Email: tom@avianevents.com

Price: $800.00

The Parrots Nest Of Maryland

4508 G Lower Beckleysville Road, Hampstead, Mary Land

Website: http://www.birdbreeders.com/bird/119312/blue-
crown-conure

Tel. No.: 410-374-1636

Email: livesaybrian@aol.com

Price: $600.00

Green Parrot Superstore

8165 S. State Rd, Goodrich, Michigan

Website: www.greenparrotsuperstore.com

Tel. No.: 810-636-9120

greenparrotsuperstore@gmail.com

Price: $695.00

Ginos Exiotic Birds

Blue Jay, CA 92317

Website: http://www.birdbreeders.com/bird/123210/scarlet-macaw

Tel. No.: 176-095-604-66

Email: Gmorrialle@gmail.com

Price: $800.00

Thea's Parrot Place

Fallbrook, California 92028

Website: www.theasparrotplace.com

Tel. No.: 760-842-3436

Email: theasparrotplace@att.net

Price: $650.00

Dusky Conures

Tail Feathers

Durand, Illinois 61024

Website: http://www.birdbreeders.com/breeder/38015/tail-feathers-durand-IL

Tel. No.: 815-248-4035

Email: tgsmall49@live.com

Price: $425.00

Featherheads

Port charlotte, Florida 33948

Website:http://www.birdbreeders.com/breeder/13627/featherheads-florida-port-charlotte-FL

Tel. No.: 813-679-4961

Price: $300.00

Golden Conures

Birds By Joe LLC

1309 Bound Brook Road, Middlesex, NJ 08846

Website: www.birdsbyjoe.com

Tel. No.: 732-764-2473

Email: service@birdsbyjoe.com

Price: Not listed

Half-Moon Conures

Thea's Parrot Place

Fallbrook, California 92028

Website: www.theasparrotplace.com

Tel. No.: 760-842-3436

Email: theasparrotplace@att.net

Price: $400.00

In A Pickle Parrots

7924 Broadview Road, Broadview Heights, Ohio 44147

Website: www.inapickleparrots.com

Tel. No.: 440-627-6477

Email: Inapickleaviary@aol.com

Price: $375.00

Maroon-Belly Conure

Above the Rainbow Aviary

Gallipolis Ferry, West Virginia 25515

Website:http://www.birdbreeders.com/breeder/10444/above-the-rainbow-aviary-gallipolis-ferry-WV

Tel. No.: 304-812-4340

Email: abovetherainbowaviary@comcast.net

Price: $300.00

Something Cheeky

Clayton, North Carolina 27520

Website: www.somethingcheeky.com

Tel. No.: 1-919-585-2241

Price: $250.00

Mitred Conures

Tweety Bird Aviary

263 Hobbs Island Road, Huntsville, AL 35803

Website: www.tweetybirdaviary.com

Tel. No.: 256-656-2019

E-mail: LBroach487@Gmail.com

Price: $400.00

Nanday Conures

Avian Events, LLC

Conyers, GA 30094

Website: www. avianevents.com

Tel. No.: 770-500-2882

Email: tom@avianevents.com

Price: $800.00

In A Pickle Parrots

7924 Broadview Road, Broadview Heights, Ohio 44147

Website: www.inapickleparrots.com

Tel. No.: 440-627-6477

Email: Inapickleaviary@aol.com

Price: $365.00

Whidbey Birds

P.O. Box 1682 Coupeville, Washington 98239

Website: www.whidbeybirds.com

Tel. No.: 360-929-2869

E-mail: whidbeybirds@msn.com

Price: $400.00

Birds Exotic

1060 S. Chester Ave. Delran, NJ 08075

Website: www.thebirdstore.com

Tel. No.: 856-764-2473

E-mail: thebirdstore@yahoo.com

Price: $499.99

Green Parrot Superstore

8165 S. State Rd, Goodrich, Michigan

Website: www.greenparrotsuperstore.com

Tel. No.: 810-636-9120

greenparrotsuperstore@gmail.com

Price: $400.00

Birds By Joe LLC

1309 Bound Brook Road, Middlesex, NJ 08846

Website: www.birdsbyjoe.com

Tel. No.: 732-764-2473

Email: service@birdsbyjoe.com

Price: $299.99

Peach-Front Conure

Thea's Parrot Place

Fallbrook, California 92028

Website: www.theasparrotplace.com

Tel. No.: 760-842-3436

Email: theasparrotplace@att.net

Price: $375.00

Pearly Conure

The Bird Lady

17044 I-20, Lindale, Texas 75771

Website: http://www.birdbreeders.com/breeder/7816/the-bird-lady-east-of-dallas-off-of-i-20-TX/reviews

Tel. No.: 956-309-0750

E-mail: debinmcallen@att.net

Price: $350.00

Something Cheeky

Clayton, North Carolina 27520

Website: www.somethingcheeky.com

Tel. No.: 1-919-585-2241

Price: $375.00

Rose-Crown Conure

Something Cheeky

Clayton, North Carolina 27520

Website: www.somethingcheeky.com

Tel. No.: 1-919-585-2241

Price: $550.00

Rosiefrons Conures

AJ'S Feathered Friends

804 N. La Fox Street. South Elgin, IL 60177

Website: www.ajspetshop.com

Tel. No.: 847-695-5624

Price: $600.00

Something Cheeky

Clayton, North Carolina 27520

Website: www.somethingcheeky.com

Tel. No.: 1-919-585-2241

Price: $375.00

Wagler Conure

Lone Palm Aviary
Loxahatchee, Florida 33470
Website: www.lpbirds.com
Tel. No.: 570-730-1366
Email: jessica@lpbirds.com
Price: $1,200.00

Jenday Conure

The Bird Lady
17044 I-20, Lindale, Texas 75771
Website: http://www.birdbreeders.com/breeder/7816/the-bird-lady-east-of-dallas-off-of-i-20-TX/reviews
Tel. No.: 956-309-0750
E-mail: debinmcallen@att.net
Price: $300.00

The Finch Farm Co.
Miami, Florida 33101
Website: www.thefinchfarm.com
Tel. No.: 877-527-5656
E-mail: jenna.thefinchfarm@gmail.com
Price: $349.95

Birdmans Baby Parrots

Chicago, Illinois 60659

Website: www.birdmansparrots.com

Tel. No.: 773-317-3785

Email: eliasnamroud@gmail.com

Price: $400.00

Featherheads

Port charlotte, Florida 33948

Website:http://www.birdbreeders.com/breeder/13627/feathe
rheads-florida-port-charlotte-FL

Tel. No.: 813-679-4961

Price: $350.00

Ara Aviaries California

Agoura Hills Los Angeles, California

Website: www.aracaris.com

Tel. No.: 805-338-3549

Email: billysaylors6@gmail.com

Price: $475.00

Thea's Parrot Place

Fallbrook, California 92028

Website: www.theasparrotplace.com

Tel. No.: 760-842-3436

Email: theasparrotplace@att.net

Price: $450.00

In A Pickle Parrots

7924 Broadview Road, Broadview Heights, Ohio 44147

Website: www.inapickleparrots.com

Tel. No.: 440-627-6477

Email: Inapickleaviary@aol.com

Price: $395.00

Ana's Parrots

East Stroudsburg, PA 18301

Website: https://www.facebook.com/PoconoAna

Tel. No.: 646-496-5005

E-mail: poconoana@yahoo.com

Price: $600.00

Parrotsrok

Skiatook, Oklahoma 74070

Website: http://parrotsrok.com/Home%20Page.html

Tel. No.: 918-289-8787

E-mail: mandmok@sbcglobal.net

Price: $350.00

Green – Cheek Conure

Above the Rainbow Aviary

Gallipolis Ferry, West Virginia 25515

Website:http://www.birdbreeders.com/breeder/10444/above-the-rainbow-aviary-gallipolis-ferry-WV

Tel. No.: 304-812-4340

Email: abovetherainbowaviary@comcast.net

Price: $275.00

Tweety Bird Aviary

263 Hobbs Island Road, Huntsville, AL 35803

Website: www.tweetybirdaviary.com

Tel. No.: 256-656-2019

E-mail: LBroach487@Gmail.com

Price: $200.00

Birdmans Baby Parrots

5668 N Lincoln Ave Chicago, Illinois

Website: www.birdmansparrots.com

Tel. No.: 773-317-3785

Price: $375.00

The Parrot's Cove

New Iberia, Los Angeles 70560

Website: theparrotcove.com

Tel. No.: 337-519-3943

E-mail: theparrotscove@theparrotcove.com

Price: $200.00

5 Oaks Aviary

Oklahoma City, Oklahoma 73150

Website: www.fiveoaksaviary.com

Tel. No.: 405-209-4312

E-mail: fiveoaksaviary@msn.com

Price: $275.00

Debbie's Birdhouse

32 East Harrison Street Tunkhannock, Pennsylvania 18657

Website: www.debbiesbirdhouse.com

Tel. No.: 570-240-7268

E-mail: Debbie57@ptd.net

Price: $275.00

The Finch Farm Co.

Miami, Florida 33101

Website: www.thefinchfarm.com

Tel. No.: 877-527-5656

E-mail: jenna.thefinchfarm@gmail.com

Price: $229.95

Linville's Aviary

Miami, Florida 33174

Website:http://www.birdbreeders.com/breeder/2920/linvilles
-aviary-miami-FL

Tel. No.: 305-968-1536

E-mail: cerbyu@aol.com

Price: $225.00

AJ'S Feathered Friends

804 N. La Fox Street. South Elgin, IL 60177

Website: www.ajspetshop.com

Tel. No.: 847-695-5624

Price: $425.00

Something Cheeky

Clayton, North Carolina 27520

Website: www.somethingcheeky.com

Tel. No.: 1-919-585-2241

Price: $350.00

Thea's Parrot Place

Fallbrook, California 92028

Website: www.theasparrotplace.com

Tel. No.: 760-842-3436

Email: theasparrotplace@att.net

Price: $280.00

Pet Paradise

35535 Euclid Avenue, Willoughby, Ohio

Website: www.petparadiseohio.com

Tel. No.: 440-942-9016

E-mail:info@petparadiseohio.com

Price: $399.99

In A Pickle Parrots

7924 Broadview Road, Broadview Heights, Ohio 44147

Website: www.inapickleparrots.com

Tel. No.: 440-627-6477

Email: Inapickleaviary@aol.com

Price: $225.00

The Bird Hut

Nashville, Tennessee 37221

Website: www.the-bird-hut.com

Tel. No.: 615-739-0631

E-mail: midtnecho@yahoo.com

Price: $200.00

Ana's Parrots

East Stroudsburg, PA 18301

Website: https://www.facebook.com/PoconoAna

Tel. No.: 646-496-5005

E-mail: poconoana@yahoo.com

Price: $450.00

Sun Conures

The Finch Farm Co.

Miami, Florida 33101

Website: www.thefinchfarm.com

Tel. No.: 877-527-5656

E-mail: jenna.thefinchfarm@gmail.com

Price: $399.95

Ginos Exiotic Birds

Blue Jay, CA 92317

Website: http://www.birdbreeders.com/bird/123210/scarlet-macaw

Tel. No.: 176-095-604-66

Email: Gmorrialle@gmail.com

Price: $500.00

Birdmans Baby Parrots

5668 N Lincoln Ave Chicago, Illinois

Website: www.birdmansparrots.com

Tel. No.: 773-317-3785

Price: $400.00

Delorce's Bird Barn

Charleston, South Carolina 29429

Website: www.delorcesbirdbarn.com

Tel. No.: 8432161553 or 8438198618

Email: brendabrinson1234@gmail.com

Price: $200.00

Toucan Jungle

Vista, CA 92084

Website: www.ToucanJungle.com

Tel. No.: 760-672-0127

Email: Chris@Toucanjungle.com

Price: $300.00

AJ'S Feathered Friends

804 N. La Fox Street. South Elgin, IL 60177

Website: www.ajspetshop.com

Tel. No.: 847-695-5624

Price: $475.00

Bill and Kennys family birds

135 Terry Road Hartford, Connecticut 06105

Website: http://www.birdbreeders.com/breeder/26465/bill-and-kennys-family-birds-hartford-CT

Tel. No.: 203 441-0366

Email:billsbirdsnbeaks@gmail.com

Price: $749.00

Linville's Aviary

Miami, Florida 33174

Website:http://www.birdbreeders.com/breeder/2920/linvilles
-aviary-miami-FL

Tel. No.: 305-968-1536

E-mail: cerbyu@aol.com

Price: $250.00

In A Pickle Parrots

7924 Broadview Road, Broadview Heights, Ohio 44147

Website: www.inapickleparrots.com

Tel. No.: 440-627-6477

Email: Inapickleaviary@aol.com

Price: $395.00

Fancy Feathers

31 Roseland Avenue, Caldwell, New Jersey

Website: www.fancyfeathersaviary.com

Tel. No.: 973-403-2900

E-mail: ddargenio@gmail.com

Price: $475.00

Kedzie Parrot Place

East Lansing, Michigan 48823

Website: www.kedzieparrotplace.com

Tel. No.: 517-204-3878

Email: kedzieparrotplace@hotmail.com

Price: $400.00

Cindy's Parrot Place

Chesapeake, Virginia 23321

Website: http://www.cindysparrotplace.com

Tel. No.: 1-844-572-7768

Email: info@cindysparrotplace.com

Price: $500.00

Birds By Joe LLC

1309 Bound Brook Road, Middlesex, NJ 08846

Website: www.birdsbyjoe.com

Tel. No.: 732-764-2473

Email: service@birdsbyjoe.com

Price: $495.00

Delorce's Bird Barn

Charleston, South Carolina 29429

Website: www.delorcesbirdbarn.com

Tel. No.: 8432161553 or 8438198618

Email: brendabrinson1234@gmail.com

Price: $200.00

c.) Local Conure Breeders in Great Britain

Here are the website links and contact details of local Conure breeders in Great Britain:

Private Advertiser

London, East London

Tel. No.: 075-507-760-59

Link: < http://www.pets4homes.co.uk/classifieds/1298410-spoon-feed-super-tamed-conurescinnamon-sold-london.html>

Price: £180

Yellow-Sided Conure

Private Advertiser

London, East London

Tel. No.: 075-507-760-59

Link: <http://www.pets4homes.co.uk/classifieds/1306097-very-tame-yellow-sided-conure-spoon-feed-london.html>

Price: £160

Sun Conure

Private Advertiser

Ashford, Kent

Tel. No.: 077-718-943-776

Link: <http://www.pets4homes.co.uk/classifieds/1281580-baby-hand-reared-sun-conures-ashford.html>

Price: £275

Private Advertiser

Glasgow, Lanarkshire

Tel. No.: 074-864-555-562

Link: <http://www.pets4homes.co.uk/classifieds/1281580-baby-hand-reared-sun-conures-ashford.html>

Price: £200

Maroon Belly Conures

Private Advertiser

London, East London

Tel. No.: 074-243-028-87

Link: < http://www.pets4homes.co.uk/classifieds/1314871-spoon-feed-maroon-belly-conures-london.html>

Price: £165

Green-Cheek Conures

Private Advertiser

Widnes, Cheshire

Tel. No.: 078-112-119-81

Link: <http://www.pets4homes.co.uk/classifieds/1305232-hand-reared-green-cheek-conures-widnes.html>
Price: £175

Private Advertiser
Newcastle Under Lyme, Staffordshire
Tel. No.: 017-826-122-95
Link: <http://www.pets4homes.co.uk/classifieds/1316927-cinnomen-green-cheeked-conures-newcastle-under-lyme.html>
Price: £225

Private Advertiser
London, East London
Tel. No.: 074-020-806-65
Link: <http://www.pets4homes.co.uk/classifieds/1279627-male-baby-green-cheek-conure-parrot-for-sale-london.html>
Price: £120

Private Advertiser
Smethwick, West Midlands
Tel. No.: 012-153-234-36
Link: < http://www.pets4homes.co.uk/classifieds/1173244-2016-baby-green-cheek-conure-for-sale-smethwick.htmll>
Price: £145

Jenday Conure

Private Advertiser

Nuneaton, Warwickshire

Tel. No.: 024-767-355-66

Link: <http://www.pets4homes.co.uk/classifieds/1307088-silly-tame-jenday-conure-nuneaton.html>

Price: £425

Dusky Headed Conures

Ashford, Kent

Tel. No.: 016-228-909-61

Link: <http://www.pets4homes.co.uk/classifieds/1306438-hen-dusky-headed-conures-ashford.html>

Price: £75

UK Breeder Websites

Hand Reared Parrots

<http://www.handrearedparrots.co.uk/>

Bird Trader

<http://www.birdtrader.co.uk/>

PreLoved

<http://www.preloved.co.uk/>

4.) Selecting a Healthy Conures

Conures on average can live for up to 20 - 40 years and more! These birds are long time companions, and its longevity highly depends on how your chosen breeders took care of them especially when they were young.

This section will give you simple tips on how you can spot a healthy conures that you can keep for life!

a.) Signs of a Healthy Conure

Look out for these signs so that you know if your prospect bird is healthy:

- The bird should be active, alert, and sociable
- It should eat and drink throughout the day
- It should have dry nostrils and bright, dry eyes
- The beak, legs, and feet should have normal appearance
- It should have a dry and clean vent
- Its feathers should be smooth and well-groomed

Chapter Five: Maintenance for Conures

Assuming that you have already bought a Conure as your pet, the responsibility that comes with it is the most crucial part of the process. You as the owner, have to provide for its basic needs so that it will be healthy and happy. In this chapter you will learn the different requirements needed for your bird such as its cage, accessories and food necessary for the maintenance of your Conure.

1.) Habitat and Environment

Conures have adapted well to human-modified habitats, such as parks and gardens in villages and towns. Like other kinds of birds, Conures should be kept in a bird-safe environment. As the owner you need to have knowledge of its habitat requirements and environmental conditions to ensure that your bird is healthy. You will find tons of information in this section regarding the maintenance your pet needs in order to keep them happy.

a.) Ideal Cage Size for Conures

Conures, like other birds, loves lots of space when it is inside its cage. A general guideline that you can follow when it comes to bird cages is that, the parrot should not have restricted movements and should be able to flap its wings without touching the sides of the cage.

It is also advisable to buy a durable cage preferably with locks to prevent them from escaping because they are naturally curious and quite naughty at times.

The cage should ideally provide room for both horizontal exercise and vertical climbing. A minimum of 24"x16"x20" (60 x 40 x 50 cm) with 0.5-0.75 in (1.3-1.9 cm) bar spacing is the recommended cage size for mini-size Conures, while a minimum of 44"x26"x40" (120 x 65 x

100 cm) with a bar space measuring 0.75-1.0 in. (1.9- 2.5 cm) is perfect for medium-sized species.

It is also advisable that the cage material uses non-toxic paint or else it can cause your pet to be poisoned by metal. It shouldn't also be made out of brass either because it contains zinc which could kill your parrot as well.

Ideally the cage should also have at least three doors. One as the main entrance and the other two should be used for food and water.

Your bird will be spending most of their lives inside the cage that's why it needs to be large so that it can also accommodate lots of toys and perches.

b.) Cage Maintenance

Your parrot's cage could affect the health of your pet so it's very important that you check it daily for any dirt, like its feces and spoiled food left in perches and cups to prevent health problems.

You should also change the cage paper every other day as well as check the metal parts & bars of your bird's cage periodically for chipped paint and rust, because your bird will most likely chew or swallow the flaked pieces.

You should be able to clean the cage thoroughly at least once every month. You could use a mild dishwashing liquid or bleach with warm water for about a minute. Then rinse all soap and bleach thoroughly with water before letting your bird inside the cage.

c.) Location of the Cage

Finding the perfect cage is just as important as knowing where to place it. As established earlier, conures loves to screech a lot, that's why you should also take that into consideration when finding a good location for your bird.

Put them in a place where they'll get to interact with people, and won't be too much of a disturbance at the same time – if in case they scream non-stop.

Put the cage at an eye level to create a sense of confidence in your bird and place the cage in a higher location so that they would feel secure just like in the wild.

Avoid placing the cage near dangerous fumes or drafts, this might kill them. Do not also place it directly in a window because the sun can cause your parrot to become ill due to too much heat. If it helps you can at least find a shade or cover for the cage, so that your bird may get just the right amount of heat during the day and feel comfortable during night time.

Finding the right location of the cage could lessen stressful situations for your bird so that they can enjoy their life with their new owner.

d.) Recommended Supplies

Now that your cage is all set and you already have an idea on where to properly place it, you need to provide supplies to meet its needs. Here are the recommended supplies that your Conures needs:

Perches

The main purpose of perches is to exercise your bird's feet; it could also prevent sores and foot related health issues in the future. In the wild, birds especially Conures, are used to transferring from one tree to another but in captivity of course they can't do that, so a great alternative is to buy them perches, preferably made out of fresh fruit tree branches. The minimum area for the perch is about ¾" - 1" (2 - 2.5 cm) in diameter.

You can buy different types of perches such as wood dowel, natural branch type, a therapeutic perch or a cement perch as well as Eucalyptus branches; just make sure that it is not poisonous.

Conures love to gnaw perches, and because of that you may have to replace it regularly. There are lots of perches you could choose from especially from online stores. These perches could also be used as ropes and swings for your pet. Do not put the perch above the bird's bowl or dishes otherwise the food and water will be contaminated.

Toys

Conures likes to chew anything, you may find yourself regularly buying and replacing new toys to keep them happy. It is recommended that you purchase toys that are easy to be destroyed, it'll be very interactive for your conure to prevent boredom. However, if you're in a tight budget, you can also buy toys that are durable so that it could last longer. There are a lot of toys online and in pet stores that you can buy for your conures.

It is not advisable to put all of the toys inside your bird's cage because it will become dirty and overcrowded. Rotate the toys at least once a week.

Dishes

Buy at least 3 sturdy dishes; one for fresh water, one for pellet or seed mix and one for fresh foods. Avoid buying plastic dishes because your Conure will most likely break it and it could also be harmful to its health. Place it away from the perches so that it would not be contaminated with bird droppings.

Formulated Diet

Some Conure owners feed their birds only with seeds, while some only provides a pellet diet; this however could limit the nutrients your pet is receiving.

Experts suggest that parrots should be given a variety of food for a balanced nutrition or what they call a formulated diet.

Conures are a very energetic and lively parrot that's why a good combination of formulated diet (seeds, fruits and vegetables) as well as a good amount of protein and other nutrients plus clean water is essential to keep their bodies healthy and active.

You will need a good supply of packaged pellet diet, to be mixed with seed. Then you can slowly add fresh foods and protein. Formulated bird food may already contain vitamins so it's not recommended that you give another one separately unless prescribed by your vet. Conversion takes about a week or so depending on your bird and how well you feed them.

Treats

Conures are known to perform different kinds of tricks, but of course, it always comes with a price! You can give your pet different types of treats such as fruits, seed and spray as well as Do-It-Yourself (DIY) treats like pretzels, popcorn or something healthy that your bird can munch on. Later in this book, you will be provided with a list of recommended treats as well as treats you should avoid.

e.) Bird Bath for Conures

Conures needs a regular bath ideally in the morning, to maintain a good skin condition. Here are some things you need to know on how to maintain your bird's hygiene and keep a healthy life.

Provide a misting bottle or a birdbath. All birds should be gently misted with a water bottle at room temperature. The spray should be sprayed up over the bird much like a shower rain, never spray the bird directly in its face.

It's important that you keep an eye in your bird while it is bathing. Bathe your Conure with clean water. Distilled water is sometimes required. Speak to your veterinarian on the best choice of water for your bird. During its misting and bathing procedures, make sure there are no drafts because it can cause respiratory issues. It may chill your bird when he is wet. Use towels and blankets, but be careful because it can catch the bird's nails and beaks in their threads.

To ensure that the oils from their skin glands, disease organisms or items such as lotions and hand creams do not transfer to your bird's feathers, wash your hands with soap and water thoroughly before handling your Conures.

Your bird may be ill if it seems to stop grooming and becomes dirty. Once you see this signs, contact your avian veterinarian immediately.

f.) Lighting and Environmental Temperature

The average room temperature for your conure should be 70-80°F (21-27°C). Also avoid drafty areas that will get direct heat from sun for any portion of the day.

Parrots also have tetra-chromic vision (4 color light vision including ultraviolet), that's why a full color light bulb must be present in the cage area. The incandescent or monochromatic light bulbs usually found in households are not a good choice for your Conures.

Cover the cage during nighttime or at least provide a shade to block out any excess light and also creates a more secure sleeping place. Be careful when using fabrics as cover because your bird might rip it with its claws or beak and could likely eat it.

Never ever place the cage in the kitchen or somewhere near cooking fumes because bird's can be very sensitive, that even a small amount of smoke can be fatal.

2.) Diet and Feeding

In the wild, Conures primarily eat palm nuts, seeds and fruits. Since these birds are very active, they will need nutrients that are rich in calories, protein and fats among others.

Fortunately, today's supplements have opened new and healthy options for pet owners. In this section you will be guided on how to properly feed your parrot and learn the feeding amount and nutritional requirements they need.

a.) Nutritional Needs of Conures

Feeding your Conure is not that complicated. However, its level of activity should be taken into consideration to meet its nutritional diet. They're not choosy eaters but like what was mentioned earlier, it is highly recommended that parrots should be given a variety of food for a balanced nutrition.

As much as possible avoid only giving the same type of food such as a pellet diet or seed diet only; it can result in nutrient deficiency and may lead to diseases due to its limited nutrients, which could also shorten the life expectancy of your parrot.

This section outlines the foods your pet will appreciate in order to meet the majority of its dietary needs.

b.) Types of Food

Seeds and Pellet

Seeds are a big part of any bird's diet; they eat seeds naturally in the wild and it is also a good source of Carbohydrates. However, seeds alone can cause complications because it is naturally fatty. Although some conures need fatty acids for their skin development, it still should be moderated. It is not advisable that you mixed seeds with pellets and feed it off right away, although a lot of people do recommend that; for best results offer seeds first for a few days, then slowly incorporate pellets into the diet until your Conures gets well adjusted.

The key is to give it in moderation. Feed them at least 1/8 - 1/4 cup of fortified parrot mix or diet, the amount may be vary depending on the size of your conure.

Fresh Vegetables

Vegetables contain Phytonutrients that enhance the body's immune system which prevents illnesses. Veggies are also a rich source of natural fiber for the body. However, keep in mind that you should feed them with vegetables in moderation to prevent diarrhea and make sure they are properly washed before feeding it to your bird.

Below is the list of highly recommended vegetables for Conures:

- Artichoke
- Asparagus
- Beets and greens
- Broccoli and greens
- Cabbage
- Carrots
- Cauliflower and greens
- Celery
- Chard
- Chickweed

- Chicory
- Chinese Cabbage
- Cucumber
- Dandelion Greens
- Edamame
- Eggplant
- Fennel and leaves, stems, seeds
- Kale
- Leeks
- Lettuce (darker is better)
- Mustard Greens
- Okra
- Peas/Snap Peas/String Beans/Snow Peas
- Peppers (all types)
- Radicchio
- Radish and greens
- Spinach
- Sweet Potato/Yam (cooked/parboiled)
- Squash (all types)
- Tomatoes (offer in moderation)
- Turnips and turnip greens
- Watercress
- Wheat Grass
- Yams

Fruits

Fruits are healthy and sweet; they also provide natural sources of sugars for the parrots. It is recommended that you only offer bite-sized fruits and do remove the pits or seeds of the fruits to prevent your Conure from choking.

Below are list of fruits that are highly recommended by veterinarians for your conure:

- Apples (no seed)
- Apricots (no seed)
- Banana
- Blackberries
- Blueberries
- Cherries (no seed)
- Coconut (feed sparingly due to fat content)
- Cranberries
- Custard Apple
- Dragon Fruit
- Figs
- Guava
- Grapefruit
- Grapes
- Kiwi Fruit
- Lemon
- Lime
- Longan
- Lychee

- Mango (no seed)
- Melon (cantaloupe, watermelon, honeydew)
- Nectarine (no seed)
- Olive (fresh)
- Oranges
- Papaya
- Passion Fruit
- Peach (no seed)
- Pear (no seed)
- Pineapple
- Plum (no seed)
- Pomegranate
- Pomelo
- Quince
- Raspberries
- Rose Hips
- Rowan Berries
- Schizandra Berries
- Starfruit
- Strawberries
- Tamarillo
- Tangerine

Important Reminder:

Offer fruits and vegetables daily or every 2-3 days. As a caution, if your conure didn't consume all the fruits you gave, remove all of its traces from the cage to avoid the risk of eating a spoiled fruit.

Vitamins

As mentioned earlier, some fortified parrot diet or parrot mix already contains essential vitamins. Before buying a good pellet mix or picking vegetables for your conure, you should keep in mind that Vitamin A is one of the most essential vitamin birds need.

Vitamin A improves vision and can also boost immunity. Eggs and meat are good sources of Vitamin A as well as different types of vegetables like carrots, kale broccoli, sweet potatoes, cantaloupe and squash. Too much or not enough of Vitamin A can potentially leave your conure vulnerable to diseases. Since conures have different types of species, it is best to consult with your avian veterinarian first to know the right amount of Vitamin A your pet needs.

Amino Acids

Conures need high levels of protein or amino acids to build their tissues, feathers, muscles and skin. Birds in general can produce its own amino acids. However, there are some amino acids such as threonine, tryptophan, leucine, lysine, methionine, phenylalanine and valine that some Conures are not able to produce or sustain in its body. Fortunately, the sources of these essential amino acids are available in today's bird diet products.

Here is the list of recommended protein for your pet Conures to feed on:

- Beans (cook small amounts as needed)
- Chicken (cooked, preferably shredded not fried)
- Eggs (cooked/hard boiled)
- Nuts (all types)
- Peanuts
- Seeds (birdseeds provide protein)
- Sprouts
- Turkey (cooked, preferably shredded)
- Meal Worms (feed it occasionally)

Calcium

Calcium's primary role is to make bones grow stronger and it also allows calcification of eggshells in birds. In captivity, you can provide calcium in the form of a cuttlebone or calcium treat that is attached inside your bird cage. You can also offer a powdered supplement such as packaged oyster shell which can be added directly to your pet's food. Follow the instructions on the supplement package. Calcium is also vital for muscle contraction, blood clotting and heart functions.

It is optional that your conures be exposed to UVB light for at least 3-4 hours a day; this may help for its optimal physiologic use of the calcium you are giving to your bird.

Water

Hydration is just as important for birds as it is for human beings especially during hot weather conditions to avoid dehydration; conures may drink 10 times its normal water intake during summer. They should be given access to clean, fresh and cool water. Do not use tap water because can cause the bird to be ill, as well as distilled water, instead use unflavored bottled drinking water or bottled natural spring water. If in case, tap water is used, treat it with a de-chlorinating treatment. Inability to provide fresh water to pet birds can cause upset stomach with unbearable stomachache.

Water is vital to maintain cells, digestion, feathers, and metabolism.

All water given to birds for drinking, as well as water used for misting, soaking or bathing must be 100% free of chlorine and heavy metals.

Treats

As mentioned earlier, you could give your parrots a reward every time they do something right like performing tricks or simply learning how to speak. You can feed them with different types of nuts such as almonds, macadamias, and walnuts. You can also give easy to digest and bite-sized fruits or Do-It-Yourself treats every now and then.

Some examples of DIY treats are carrot muffins (minus the sugar), popcorn, corn, unsalted pretzel sticks with fruits and brown rice with berries. They will surely love something appetizing to eat and this is also a positive reinforcement for the bird especially during training them.

c.) Toxic Foods to Avoid

Some foods are specifically toxic for your Conures or any type of birds in general. Make sure that your bird never gets to eat one of the toxic items below and ensure that an avian veterinary checks your bird every now and then. These harmful foods is as important as selecting the right supplements and food items for your bird.

The following list of foods is highly toxic for your Conures:

- Onions
- Alcohol
- Mushrooms
- Tomato Leaves
- Caffeine

- Dried Beans
- Parsley
- Chocolate (highly allergic)
- Avocados
- Junk Food
- Apple and Cherry Seeds
- Lettuce
- Milk and Dairy Products
- French fries,
- Marbled meat
- Peanut Butter
- Butter

3.) *Handling and Training Conures*

There would be instances that your pet will be out of its cage, especially for Conures. These birds are very active and naturally playful. However, it's also important to keep in mind on how to properly handle and train your Conure so that it will not cause harm to itself and to people as well.

In this section, you'll learn some guidelines on how to confidently handle your parrot as well as some tips on trimming its nails, wings and beaks to maximize its balance, abilities and flying potential.

a.) Tips for Taming Your Conure

Taming your conure is the first thing to do before teaching them some cool tricks.

The flipside of owning a macaw conure is that they have quite a reputation for having a witty attitude and really loves to play tricks on people, in some cases they even tend to bite when feel threatened. The key is to figure out the level of your bird's comfort zone and remove it so that you could have a great bonding experience together. Here are some tips on how to do tame your conure:

- Start by slowly touching your parrot in its beak. Carefully move your hand closer and closer towards its beak. If the parrot reacts or moves away, stop for a while.
- Wait for it to calm down, then take your hand away and give a treat.
- Practices repeating this procedure until you are able to fully touch its beak. Your conure will eventually tolerate you in touching its beak and once you do, you can also scratch their beak. Just be extra careful when doing it, their beaks are sharp and really strong, but you have to conquer your fear if you want to get along with them!

b.) Tips for Training Your Conure

Now that you and your conure quite get along already, strengthen your relationship by training them some basic lessons.

Training a conure is not that hard to do, in fact it can be a fun and rewarding bonding experience for you and your feathered friend! There are lots of pet owners out there who have properly trained and raised a well-behaved conure. They are clever creatures by nature, that is why they can absorb information very quickly and easily as long as you do it right.

Trust is the most important key in training your parrot. The first thing you need to do is to be able to establish a solid connection and rapport between you and your pet.

This section will provide some guidelines you can follow in getting your bird well behaved and disciplined. Are you ready? Read on!

Stepping Up is a basic skill your parrot should learn, to find out how to do this follow the tips below:

- A good way to pacify your bird into your hands without being forceful is to try and make your parakeet step up onto a handheld perch.
- Slowly and progressively begin training it to step up on your hand. If you are afraid of being bitten then

wear gloves, but you may want to get rid of it eventually because it might still encourage them to bite you because they can chew the leather.

- Hold your hand in a short distance away from your parrot so that when it tries to step into the target stick, it will have no choice but to step into your hand.
- Keep practicing until your parrot won't need your stick anymore. It will get accustomed and comfortable whenever you command it to step up in your finger

Grooming Your Conure

a.) Trimming Your Conure's Nails

Like many parrots, conures have a sharp, needle-like nails because they do a lot of climbing in the wild, and they also use these nails to dig into wood to keep them secure.

Unclipped nails can dig into the skin, leaving scratches or painful wounds to a person, only clipped to a point that the bird can perch securely and does not bother you when the bird is perched on your hand. Many people have their conure's nails clipped to the point that it becomes dull and the bird can no longer grip a perch firmly.

This can result to becoming more clumsy and nervous because it cannot move without slipping. This nervousness can develop into fear biting and panic attacks.

Another tip is only use a styptic powder on your bird's nails, not the skin!

b.) Trimming Your Conure's Beaks

Although, conures can pretty much maintain its beak's from deformity on its own, it's still important that you keep them in good condition. They are very fond of chewing and pecking everything they can get into. That's why it may eventually become dull which could also lead to deformation if not properly cared for.

Consult a qualified veterinarian to show you the proper way in trimming your pet's beaks. You can also check out several grooming items such as lava and mineral blocks that are available in your local pet store, to keep their beaks in great shape.

c.) Clipping a Conure's Wings

Birds are design to fly, young conures can be fairly clumsy and flying gives them confidence as well as agility, stamina, and muscle tone.

Before clipping their wings, make sure that your conures are flying, maneuvering and landing well already. If they do not learn how to properly land by lifting their wings and flaring their tail, then when they are clipped, they could injure themselves and could also break their beak or keel bone.

Consult a qualified veterinarian to show you the proper way in clipping a bird's wings. A certain amount of flight feathers will be removed while leaving the smaller balancing feathers inside the wing closer to the body uncut.

Chapter Six: Breeding Conures

If you decided to buy two conures, for instance a male and female and keep them together, you should definitely prepare for the possibility of breeding, unless it's the same gender, otherwise you're going to be caught off guard!

If you are interested in breeding your conure, this chapter will give you a wealth of information about the processes and phases of its breeding and you will also learn how to properly breed them on your own. This is not for everyone but if you want to have better understanding about how these birds procreate, then you should definitely not miss this part! On the contrary if you are interested in becoming a reputable breeder, then this is a must read chapter for you.

1.) Basic Conure Breeding Info

Before deciding if you truly want to become a breeder, you should at least have prior knowledge on their basic reproduction process and breeding. This section will inform you on how these creatures procreate.

a.) Sexual Dimorphism

Conures are not sexually dimorphic; males and females are visually identical, although the females sometimes have a narrower eye ring than the males. You can only determine it through DNA analysis, which uses sample blood or feathers. Although, some breeders claim that they can distinguish if the bird is male or female because of its features, it is still indefinite unless it's DNA is tested.

DNA Sexing or Surgical Sexing can also provide additional information on its sexual maturity and capability to reproduce. It is inexpensive and convenient so if you like to know more about your bird's sexuality you should definitely give it a try. Some veterinarians might also try chromosomal analysis on your macaw to determine its gender.

b.) Mating and Reproduction

Conures are typically monogamous when it comes to finding its mate. The breeding period for these birds usually occurs year-round and once they start breeding, they'll continuously breed every year.

In terms of reproduction, mini-conures reach their sexual maturity as early as 2 years old, while medium-sized ones becomes mature at 3 – 4 years old; females' clutch size ranges from 2 – 5 eggs with a maximum 7 – 12 eggs and incubation lasts for about 23 – 27 days.

The chicks become independent and leave the nest in when they reach approximately 50 days.

It is highly recommended that you provide an additional 20% increase on fatty seeds as well as their intake of vitamin supplements and proteins such as hard-boiled egg and shredded chicken during the breeding process.

It's also important to note that the incubation temperature should be kept between 37.2° - 37.3 °C (99.1°- 99.2°F) and humidity level should be at about 50 – 55% before the eggs are hatched.

2.) The Conure Breeding Process

In order to have a clear sketch of how Conures reproduce, this section will show you the breeding process and the information you need to know, so that your pets can successfully procreate.

a.) Selecting Conures for Breeding

For you to select a healthy, fertile and active parrot it is recommended that your parrot undergoes clinical examination by a veterinarian. This is essential to determine if your parrot is capable of reproduction or not and at the same time it can prevent diseases that could be transmitted to the coming flock.

b.) Setting up a Good Nesting Environment

Conures in the wild usually nest in tree hollows or cliff openings; in captivity, you need to set up a nice environment to replicate that natural breeding and dwelling place so that they can successfully mate and create healthy clutches. The nest box size should ideally measure 12"x12"x12" (30 x 30 x 30 cm).

Keep in mind that the box should be three times the size of your conure. It is highly recommended that the nest box is wide so that your conures can have lots of space to move around and that it should ideally be made out of oak wood or metal.

The nest box should have a circular or round entrance hole that has an opening of about 3 inches (7.62 cm). Make sure that a strong wire is attached to the outside walls of the nest to prevent from escaping. To be able to help stabilize the eggs you can add about 2 inches of suitable nest box litter at the bottom of the box. Providing this may also be beneficial in absorbing the droppings from the chicks

c.) Nesting Materials

If you prefer to build your own nest box instead of buying one, you have to make sure that the materials you use are strong so that it will have a good foundation otherwise, your conures could easily destroy it.

You should also put short pieces of wood or wood chips inside the box for your birds to chew; you can also give them bite-sized timber. Just make sure that it is large enough to not let the small chicks accidentally ingest it. This may help the breeders increase the percentage of fertile eggs and synchronize their breeding cycle as well.

d.) Brooding and Incubation

Conures breed all year round but breeding season usually happens around spring time. Smaller species of conures reach their sexual maturity as early as 2 years old, while medium-sized or larger ones becomes mature at 3 – 4 years old; females' clutch size ranges from 2 – 5 eggs with a maximum 7 – 12 eggs and incubation lasts for about 23 – 27 days.

Generally, there is a 2 – 3 days interval for female conures after the first egg is laid. The chicks become independent and leave the nest in usually in 1 – 2 months or approximately 50 days.

e.) Hatching

On average, the eggs hatch in about 24 – 48 hours after the incubation period for all types of conures and it takes about 1 – 2 months before the young conures leave the nest. Consult your vet on the suitable type of diet and vitamins or supplements needed for your baby conures.

5.) Hybridization of Conures

Hybrids are the offspring of parents of different species, subspecies or races. Cross-breeding is quite common especially within genera. Hybrids are a wonderful mixture of colors and they have interracial qualities, which makes it way more expensive than regular conures, so it's favorable for pet traders. Some examples of hybrid conures are the Sun Conure and Jenday Conure.

Generally, there are three generations of hybrid in parrots; the first-generation hybrid is a crossing of two natural occurring species. The second-generation hybrid is a natural conure specie combined with a first-generation hybrid, while the third-generation hybrid is the product of crossing hybrid conures (either first or second generation).

Some bird enthusiasts and experts are against the practice of hybridization because it affects the naturally occurring bird population. If you would like to breed a hybrid conure, it is best to consult with your avian veterinarian first to check if your parrot has the capability to reproduce and to also avoid diseases.

a.) List of Hybrid Conure Breeders in United States

Below are the lists of hybrid conure breeders in United States, please be reminded that these conures may be more expensive than their usual price. The rarer the species, the more expensive it could be. The availability and price of these birds may also vary.

Fancy Feathers

31 Roseland Avenue, Caldwell, New Jersey

Website: www.fancyfeathersaviary.com

Tel. No.: 973-403-2900

E-mail: ddargenio@gmail.com

Delorce's Bird Barn

(Harlequin macaw)

Charleston, South Carolina 29429

Website: www.delorcesbirdbarn.com

Tel. No.: 8432161553 or 8438198618

Email: brendabrinson1234@gmail.com

Green Parrot Superstore

(Ruby Macaw)

8165 S. State Rd, Goodrich, Michigan

Website: www.greenparrotsuperstore.com

Tel. No.: 810-636-9120

greenparrotsuperstore@gmail.com

Ana's Parrots

East Stroudsburg, PA 18301

Website: https://www.facebook.com/PoconoAna

Tel. No.: 646-496-5005

E-mail: poconoana@yahoo.com

Cindy's Parrot Place

Chesapeake, Virginia 23321

Website: http://www.cindysparrotplace.com

Tel. No.: 1-844-572-7768

Email: info@cindysparrotplace.com

Birds By Joe LLC

(Ruby Macaw)

1309 Bound Brook Road, Middlesex, NJ 08846

Website: www.birdsbyjoe.com

Tel. No.: 732-764-2473

Email: service@birdsbyjoe.com

Avian Events, LLC

(Shamrock Macaw)

Conyers, GA 30094

Website: www. avianevents.com

Tel. No.: 770-500-2882

Email: tom@avianevents.com

Chapter Seven: Keeping Conures Healthy

You as the owner should be aware of the potential threats and diseases that could harm the wellness of your Conures. Just like human beings, you need to have knowledge on these diseases so that you can prevent it from happening in the first place. You will find tons of information on the most common problems that may affect your bird including its causes, signs and symptoms, remedies and prevention.

1.) Common Health Problems

In this section, you will learn about the diseases that may affect and threaten your Conure's wellness. Learning these diseases as well as its remedies is vital for you and your bird so that you could prevent it from happening or even help with its treatment in case they caught one.

Below are some of the most common health problems that occur specifically to conure parrots. You will learn some guidelines on how these diseases can be prevented and treated as well as its signs and symptoms.

Conure Pox

Conure pox is the single deadliest disease that acquired by conures. It is caused by an Avian Poxvirus infection and it causes real damage to conures and scarred it for life.

a.) Cause and Effect

The virus is usually transmitted through a direct contact with birds carrying the virus. Biting insects or any contaminated surfaces may spread the disease even further and may make the pain worse.

b.) Signs and Symptoms

The thickening of the eyes by mucous membranes is a sign that your conure is a carrier of the virus. It manifests through a wet form of the pox that affects, mouth, gullet, and upper and lower respiratory systems.

c.) Treatment and Remedy

Veterinarians typically recommend 10,000 units of Vitamin A which are given by injection. Antibiotics are also given to treat secondary infections and a Mercurochrome solution is given to treat their mucous-thickened eyes. Consult an avian veterinarian immediately.

E – Coli

Another common illness that affects conures is a bacteria called E-Coli. It is very rampant among psittacine birds.

a.) Cause and Effect

E-Coli is a gram-negative bacteria found in guts of birds that are considered abnormal; this bacteria is highly capable of causing diseases especially if it reaches into the bird's bloodstream, respiratory system, and reproductive system or if the carrier parrot is under a stressful situation.

b.) Signs and Symptoms

Coliform infections are the main cause of deaths in most conures, the E-Coli bacteria weakens the bird's digestive and respiratory system most of the time. A sudden loss appetite and difficulty in breathing may be a sign that your bird is suffering from this bacteria.

c.) Treatment and Remedy

Veterinarians usually have to determine first if these bacteria are the disease causing agents or merely a secondary infection through a culture testing before treating it with antibiotics or other necessary medicines.

Proventricular Dilation Disease

This disease is commonly known as Wasting Disease, it is rampant among conure species. It is an inflammatory wasting disease caused by a virus called Avian BornaVirus (ABV), which is mostly found in Psittacine species specially in Conures. It primarily affects the Central Nervous System and multiple organs such as liver, kidneys, heart, brain, peripheral blood vessels, lungs and gastrointestinal tract.

a.) Cause and Effect

It is classified as a sporadic disease that has a very rare kind of attack to a bird's immune system. Unlike other virus which attacks the whole cell then move to another cell,

ABV does not destroy the cells which leave the infected ones very little damage. Since the cells are not destroyed the immune system cannot detect it and thus the virus stays within the bird for an indefinite amount of time, which eventually weakens the immune system and results in continuous infections throughout the parrot's life.

c.) Diagnosis

Avian veterinarians have difficulties in detecting the virus because of other infections it can bring to the bird's health. The ABV does not show-up in the test results and there are other viruses similar to ABV which may also lead in the assumption that the bird is not a carrier even if it is.

d.) Signs and Symptoms

ABV is also an asymptomatic virus, which means that there are no signs that the bird might be infected or a carrier. However, sometimes you can notice it if your pet experienced instances of mild disorders such as moaning, feather-plucking or self-mutilation to severe illness such as head tremors, paralysis, seizures or other sudden sickness due to infected organs in the body.

e.) Treatment and Remedy

Veterinarians classified the severity of disease and level of impact to different stages such as low-to-moderate symptoms to severe and chronic stages.

Parrots in the early stages are given treatment to prevent the virus from spreading and eventually curing it. Although, this virus can be controlled and has a remedy, it's important that your bird always goes for checkup and undergo medical tests every now and then especially if it was diagnosed with the virus before.

Coacal Papilloma

It is caused by a virus infection similar to warts in other animals and it is transmitted through direct contact. These tiny tumors usually appear in the vent area of a conure where it can eventually block the fecal area of making it hard for the bird to defecate if it grows large enough.

a.) Treatment

The recommended treatment for this is a laser surgery. As a remedy veterinarians also advised owners to offer Jalapino peppers to prevent and control papilloma in birds. Consult your avian vet on the right amount of peppers to feed to your conure.

Psittacosis or Parrot Fever

It is a zoonotic infectious disease caused by an unknown organism whose natural hosts are birds such as Conures.

a.) Cause and Effect

It is an airborne disease and it can also be spread via the bird's feces. This disease is highly contagious. Before acquiring a Conure, it's important that your bird goes through a Psittacosis test because this type of infection can also potentially harm a human being.

b.) Signs and Symptoms

The worst thing about this disease is that it is asymptomatic, which means symptoms does not appear or cannot be detected easily, you will never know when it could happen and if the bird is a carrier. Nevertheless, watch out for these possible signs that your pet might be having Psittacosis:

- Difficulty in breathing (due to Respiratory infections with airsac)
- Sneezing
- Runny eyes
- Congestion

- Liver disease might occur (and can progress rapidly to death)

c.) Diagnosis of Psittacosis

As mentioned earlier, this type of disease is asymptomatic that sometimes even a psittacosis test could not detect the disease. Identifying organisms in the feces is done in most cases.

d.) Treatment and Remedy

This disease is treated with a tetracycline based antibiotic given for about 45 days to eliminate the carrier state, although some veterinarians believe that the antibiotic does not necessarily remove the carrier state.

Pacheco's Disease

This disease is caused by a herpes virus which attacks the liver and results in acute liver failure. It is very contagious and highly fatal to most birds.

a.) Diagnosis

Diagnosis is done via necropsy which detects microscopic evidences of the virus found in the liver.

b.) Treatment and Remedy

Unfortunately, there is no guaranteed antibiotic or remedy for this disease, the best you could do is to minimize the spread of the virus through intensive care and some antiviral medication.

Aspergillosis

It is a respiratory disease caused by the fungus called *Aspergillus*, which is found in warm and moist environments.

a.) Cause and Effect

The microscopic spores of Aspergillus are an airborne transmitted disease. The fungus does not cause the disease per se but if your bird does not have a healthy immune system it can cause illness.

It increases the chances of the spores being inhaled by your bird if the environment has poor ventilation and sanitation, dusty conditions, and in close confinements.

Other predisposing factors include poor nutrition, other medical conditions in the respiratory system and prolonged use of antibiotics or corticosteroids, which eventually weakens the immune system. Aspergillosis is more common in parrots than other pet birds.

b.) Signs and Symptoms

There are two kinds of Aspergillosis, it's either acute or chronic, both of which attacks the respiratory system.

Acute Aspergillosis signs and symptoms include:

- Severe difficulty in breathing
- Cyanosis (a bluish coloration of mucous membranes and/or skin)
- Decreased or loss of appetite
- Frequent drinking and urination

Chronic Aspergillosis symptoms include:

- White nodules appear through the respiratory tissue
- Large numbers of spores enter the bloodstream
- Infection in the kidneys, skin, muscle, gastrointestinal tract, liver, eyes, and brain

Other signs of Aspergillosis may include:

- Rapid breathing
- Exercise intolerance
- Change in syrinx (voice box); reluctance to talk
- Discharged and clogging of Nares
- Tremors

- Seizures or paralysis
- Green discoloration in the urates may be seen
- Enlarged liver
- Gout (painful, inflamed joints due to urate deposits)
- Depression and lethargy

c.) Diagnosis of Aspergillosis

Aspergillosis is generally difficult to detect until complete diagnosis. Do not compromise respiratory infections, consult the veterinarian immediately.
Here are some of the tests that your Conures need to undergo through for diagnosis

- Radiographs (a complete blood count)
- Endoscopy (used to view lesions in the syrinx or trachea)
- PCR testing for the presence of Aspergillus

d.) Treatment and Remedy

Always consult a veterinarian first to know the right remedy for your bird. There are reports that the antifungal drug Itraconazole may also be toxic to Conure parrots than to other bird species. Another antifungal drug called Amphotericin B may be administered orally, topically, by injection, or nebulizing. Consult your vet for proper guidance. Surgery may also be performed to remove accessible lesions. Supportive care is often needed such as oxygen, supplemental heat, tube feeding, and treatment of underlying conditions.

e.) Prevention

Maintaining a good husbandry and diet can highly prevent outbreaks of Aspergillosis.

Below are some tips you can do to ensure that your bird is free from such a deadly disease:

- Keep your bird in a well-ventilated environment.
- Always clean the food and water dishes
- Thoroughly clean cages, toys, perches and other accessories at least once a month.
- Replace substrate (material lining the cage bottom) regularly
- Offer a good nutrition, such as the right combination of fruits, vegetables and seeds

Psittacine Beak and Feather Disease (PBFD)

PBFD is a viral condition that is responsible for damage to the beak, feathers and nails as well as the immune system of infected birds. These are very common in parrots between 6 months and 3 years of age.

a.) Signs and symptoms

PBFD typically affects the feathers of infected birds as well as its beak and nails over time. Here are some signs and symptoms that your pet might have PBFD.

- Feathers are short, fragile, malformed, and prone to bleeding and breaking. Birds may first lose their the white, fine powder produced by specialized feathers to help maintain feather health when this happens more abnormal feathers will eventually develop.
- Beak has become glossy rather than the more typical matte appearance
- Nails and beak becomes brittle and malformed
- Significant loss of feathers (as the follicles become damaged)
- Loss of appetite (especially in young conures)
- Regurgitation or continuous vomiting

b.) Diagnosis

Veterinarians will likely perform a PCR test to confirm the diagnosis. This test uses advanced techniques to look for the virus' DNA.

Most of the time PCR only needs a blood sample, but your veterinarian may also need to take a swab from your bird's mouth and vent.

Other kinds of test may include:

- Complete blood count and a chemistry panel tests.
- DNA test for specifically for PBFD

c.) Treatment

The majority of clinically affected birds will die within a few months to a year because there are no antiviral drugs available to fight the virus. Your avian veterinarian can only help keep your bird comfortable because this condition is painful for the bird and it also allows secondary infections to take hold. Some birds may survive for a few months they will ultimately die from this disease.

d.) Prevention

The only thing breeders and pet owners can do to prevent this deadly virus is to take pro-active steps but since you can't help the birds mingle with other birds as they travel from wholesaler to retail pet distributors to your home the best solution is to have your bird examined by an avian veterinarian and allow diagnostic testing.

It is also wise to take your bird for a yearly exam to make sure it stays healthy. Yearly exams can catch small issues before they get worse.

Tracheal Mites

Tracheal Mites are quite common in birds because it can infiltrate the bird's entire respiratory tract and the severity of the infection can vary greatly. Birds with mild infections may not show any signs but severe infections may produce symptoms including trouble breathing, wheezing or clicking sounds, open-mouth breathing, and excessive salivation.

a.) Cause and Effect

This disease can be transmitted through close contact with an infected bird and through airborne particles. It can also be passed through contaminated food or drinking water.

b.) Diagnosis

It is quite difficult to diagnose if your conure has tracheal mites, veterinarians often recommend performing a tracheal swab to check under a microscope for further evalutation.

c.) Signs and Symptoms

Common signs include sneezing, wheezing or difficulty in breathing. Continuous bobbing of the tail while breathing is also a sign that your conure may have a respiratory problem. Tracheal mites also overlap with a number of other infections that has the same symptoms, so you need to make sure you have an accurate diagnosis.

d.) Treatment and Remedy

Medications are available to treat the disease, though dosage can be tricky and many birds die from tracheal mites. It is best to consult your veterinarian first before getting any treatment options available for tracheal mites.

Other common types of disorders and injuries in conures include:

- Constricted Toe
- Crop Burn
- Crop Punctures
- Dehydration
- Splay Leg
- Ruptured Air Sac
- Slipped Tendon
- Split Sternum
- Scissors Beak
- Sour and Slow Crop
- Sinusitis
- Salmonellosis
- Nasal Discharge
- Gout
- Beak and Feather Syndrome

2. Recommended Tests

Here are the recommended tests your conures should undergo through to detect potential diseases and further evaluate its health condition so that it can be prevented and treated as soon as possible.

For young conures, you might want to do a CBC or **Complete Blood Count**; this is a general test for birds and even humans to test for any internal infections. Another test is called **Chlamydophila Immunoassay**; this is a diagnosis exam to check if your bird might be carrying a contagious parrot fever, which is also potentially harmful to humans. You might also want to do a **Culture diagnosis** to detect if there are any bacterial infections in your young conures.

For adult conures, a CBC and Culture diagnosis should be done regularly as prescribed by your avian veterinarian as well as a full body X-ray usually with gas sedation for further evaluation of your pet's condition. If there are any signs of illness, veterinarians will recommend further tests to identify your bird's potential disease.

3.) Signs of Possible Illnesses

For you to keep your conures healthy, you need to monitor them to ensure that they are in good condition, however there will come a time that your bird will get sick.

Here are some early warning signs that your conure could be potentially ill.

- **Activity** – Is your bird sleeping when it normally does not? Or being quiet when it normally isn't? Is there a decreased in food and water intake or not being able to eat at all like before?
- **Droppings** (feces) - Are there any change in urates (white part) or feces that is lasting more than 1-2 days?
- **Diarrhea** - Have you found undigested food in your bird's feces? Their droppings should have the three distinct parts (green/brown, white and liquid urine). If you think your conure has diarrhea, contact your vet immediately.
- **Weight loss** - Does your bird feels "light" when you pick it up? That maybe a sign of weight loss because the Keel bone becomes more prominent.
- **Feathers** – Is there a continuous presence of pinfeathers? It may be dull in color, broken, bent and fluffed up feathers.
- **Sneezing** – Is there a discharge in the nostrils when your bird sneezes? Look for stained feathers over the nares or crusty material in or around the nostrils.
- **Vomiting** – Has your pet been vomiting for quite a long period of time already? Conures and all birds

regurgitate occasionally as a sign of "affection" but it could also indicate a crop infection

- **Respiratory** – Are there signs of respiratory distress like tail bobbing up and down with each breath, a change in breathing sounds, and wheezing or clicking noise when it inhales?
- **Balance** – Has your bird been falling off its perch and huddling at the bottom of cage? It is a sign that it's losing its balance.
- **Eyes** – Does it appear dull? Is there a redness/swelling and loss of feathers around the eyes?
- **Feet** – Is it scaly or flaky? Does it have sores on the bottom of the feet?
- **Head** – Have you noticed excessive head bobbing and shaking?
- **Beak** – Is your bird's beak swelling?
- **Behavior** – does your bird sits on the floor of its cage or habitat? Does it favor one foot over the other?

When these things happen, contact your avian veterinarian immediately. Do not compromise your bird's health; prevention is always better than cure.

Chapter Eight: Conure Checklist

Congratulate yourself! You are now on your way to becoming a very well-informed and pro-active Conure owner! Finishing this book is a huge milestone for you and your future or present pet bird, but before this ultimate guide comes to a conclusion, keep in mind the most important things you have acquired through reading this book.

This chapter will outline the summary of what you have learned, the do's and dont's as well as the checklist you need to tick off to ensure that you and your Conure lived happily ever after!

1.) Basic Information

- **Taxonomy**: phylum *Chordata*, class *Aves*, order *Psittaciformes*, family *Psittacidae*, Subfamily *Arinae*, Tribe *Arini*.
- **Distribution**: Latin America, South and Central America, Caribbean
- **Habitat**: Tropical dry forests, dry savannahs
- **Lifestyle**: Flock Oriented
- **Anatomical Adaptations**:
- **Breeding Season**: All year round; spring
- **Eggs**: 2 – 5 eggs
- **Incubation Period**: 23 – 27 days
- **Sexual Maturity** : 2 – 3 years old
- **Average Size**: 22 cm – 48 cm (9 – 19 in)
- **Average Weight**: 73 – 190 grams
- **Wingspan**: 6 – 162 cm (2 – 23 in)
- **Coloration**: red, green, orange, white, yellow, and brown
- **Sexual Dimorphism**: Sexually dimorphic
- **Diet**: Seeds, Insects, Fruit, Nuts (Omnivore)
- **Sounds**: Vocal Communicator
- **Interaction**: Highly Social
- **Lifespan**: 20 – 40 years

2.) Cage Set-up Guide

- **Minimum Cage Dimensions**: 24"x16"x20" (60 x 40 x 50 cm) for small conures; 44"x26"x40" (120 x 65 x 100 cm) medium-sized conures.
- **Cage Shape**: the bigger, the better. Never purchase a round cage.
- **Bar Spacing**: 0.5-0.75 in (1.3-1.9 cm) for small conures; 0.75-1.0 in. (1.9- 2.5 cm) for medium-sized conures.
- **Required Accessories**: food and water dishes, perches, grooming and cleaning materials, cuttlebone, toys
- **Food/Water Dish**: 3 sturdy dishes; one for fresh water, one for pellet/seed mix, and one for fresh foods. Do not buy dishes made out of plastic
- **Perches**: at least 3 different perches; wood dowel, natural branch type, a therapeutic perch or a cement perch or any fresh fruit tree branches
- **Recommended Toys**: rotate at least 3 different toys; rope toys, stainless steel bells, swings etc.
- **Bathing Materials**: misting bottle; bath tub
- **Nests Materials**: nest box made out of wood, oak or metal
- **Recommended Temperature Range**: 37.2° - 37.3 °C (99.1°- 99.2°F)

- **Lighting:** full color light bulb must be present in the cage area. Do not use incandescent or monochromatic light bulbs.

3.) Nutritional Information

- **Types of Recommended Food:**
- **Seeds:** 1/8 - 1/4 cup of fortified parrot seed mix
- **Fresh Fruits and Vegetables:** makes up about 15 to 20% of a Conure's diet. Offer fruits and vegetables daily or every 2 - 3 days.
- **Supplements:** Calcium usually found in the form of a cuttlebone or Calcium treat. Powdered supplement such as packaged oyster shell can be added directly to your pet's food.
- **Amino Acids:** makes up about 20% of a Conure's diet.
- **Carbohydrates:** makes up about 10% of a Conure's diet (nuts, seeds, corn etc.)
- **Water:** clean, fresh and cool water; unflavored bottled drinking water or bottled natural spring water

4.) Breeding Information

- **Sexual Dimorphism:** They are not sexually dimorphic; gender can be identified through DNA sexing or chromosomal analysis.

- **Seasonal Changes**: breeding season usually begins in spring, around March to April.
- **Sexual Maturity**: 2 – 3 years old
- **Nest Box Size**: 12"x12"x12" (30 x 30 x 30 cm)
- **Egg Laying**: female lays eggs an average of 2 – 5 eggs with an interval of 2 – 3 days.
- **Clutch Size**: about 2 clutches per year
- **Incubation Period**: 23 – 27 days
- **Hatching**: takes about 24 – 28 days to hatch
- **Chick Independence**: 1 – 2 months (50 days)

5.) Do's and Dont's

- Do keep them busy and happy;
- Do feed them a variety of nutritious food
- Do train them well to maximize their intelligence
- Do provide a clean and healthy environment
- Do give them time and commitment
- Do care for them when they feel ill
- Do provide plenty of toys inside the cage
- Do bond with them and let them out of the cage once in a while so that they can be exposed outside
- Do not use sandpaper covered perches or floor paper. It can cause severe damage to your bird's feet

- Do not use "bird disks" or "mite disks". These may harm your bird. See your avian veterinarian if you suspect parasites.
- Do not use bird gravel. Bird gravel is used for birds that do not crack the hull or shell of the seeds they eat. It causes severe impactions, which are often fatal. Gravel only benefits doves and pigeons definitely not parrots
- Do not use negative reinforcement during training because it is not effective
- Don't let conures fall. It may contribute in developing respiratory problems and damages organs due to impact. Train them how to fly instead!
- Do not let your conures get near to the following household items to prevent causes of accidents:

  - Ceiling or electric fans
  - Cooking oil
  - Leg chains
  - Toxic Fumes
  - Wood shavings
  - Toxic houseplants
  - Pesticides
  - Lead or zinc materials
  - Air fresheners
  - Scented candles
  - Sandpaper-covered perches
  - Tobacco and Cigarette smoke

Chapter Nine: Relevant Websites

Finishing this book doesn't mean that you should stop learning! This chapter provides you a wealth of references online that you could check out every now and then so that you can be updated when it comes to taking care of your Conures. You can also find the websites you need to visit especially in buying cages and supplies for your pet.

1. Conure Cage Links

Here is the recommended list of websites for you to choose from when buying cages both in United States and Great Britain.

United States Links:

Custom Cages
<https://www.customcages.com/catalogsearch/result/?q=conure>

Bird Cages 4 Less
<http://birdcages4less.com/page/B/CTGY/Small_Bird_Cages>

Bird Cages Now
<http://www.birdcagesnow.com/conures/>

Pet Solutions
<http://www.petsolutions.com/C/Bird-Cages-Carriers.aspx>

Pets at Home
<http://www.petsathome.com/shop/en/pets/bird-and-wildlife/bird-cages>

Overstock

<http://www.overstock.com/Pet-Supplies/Bird-Cages-Houses/3643/cat.html>

Great Britain Links:

Cages World

<http://www.cagesworld.co.uk/f/Parrot_Cages/products::bird_type:Conure.htm>

Northern Parrots (Small and Large Conures)

<http://www.northernparrots.com/small-conures-deptb109/?category=147>

<http://www.northernparrots.com/large-conures-deptb108/?category=147>

Pebble – Home and Garden

<https://www.pebble.co.uk/compare.html?q=Conure+cage>

Seapets

<https://www.seapets.co.uk/bird-supplies/bird-cages/parrot-cages>

2. Conure Cage Accessories and Supplies

Here is the recommended list of websites for you to choose from when buying accessories such as toys, perches, dishes and other necessary supplies for your pet.

United States Links:

King's Cages

<http://www.kingscages.com/SearchResults.aspx?txtSearch=Conures&x=0&y=0>

Doctors Foster and Smith – Toys

<http://www.drsfostersmith.com/bird-supplies/bird-toys/conure-to-amazon-toys/ps/c/5059/5648/5753>

Fun Time Birdy - Toys

<http://www.funtimebirdy.com/patoyse.html>

Pet Mountain – Cleaning Supplies

< http://www.petmountain.com/category/311/1/bird-cage-cleaning-supplies.html>

PetSmart – Bowls, Feeders

<http://www.petsmart.com/bird/bowls-feeders/cat-36-catid-400014>

Wind City Parrot - Accessories

<http://www.windycityparrot.com/All_c_711.html>

Pet Solutions - Breeding Supplies

<http://www.petsolutions.com/C/Bird-Breeding-Supplies.aspx>

Bird Cages 4 Less - Perches

<http://birdcages4less.com/page/B/CTGY/Bird_Perches>

Pets at Home – Health Care Products

<http://www.petsathome.com/shop/en/pets/bird-and-wildlife/bird-healthcare-products>

Overstock - Accessories

<http://www.overstock.com/Pet-Supplies/Bird-Accessories/3646/cat.html>

Great Britain Links:

Cages World - Accessories

<http://www.cagesworld.co.uk/c/Bird_Cage_Accessories.htm>

Parrot Essentials - Accessories

<http://www.parrotessentials.co.uk/>

Parrotize UK – Parrot Stands and Covers

<http://parrotize.co.uk/products/parrot-stands/>

Seapets – Bird Toys

<https://www.seapets.co.uk/bird-supplies/bird-toys>

ZooPlus – Accessories
<http://www.zooplus.co.uk/shop/birds/cage_accessories>

3. Conure Diet and Food Links

Here is the recommended list of websites for you to choose from when buying seeds and parrot food for your pet.

United States Links:

Pet Mountain
< http://www.petmountain.com/category/314/1/conure-food.html>

Harrison's Bird Food

<http://www.harrisonsbirdfoods.com/>

Nature Chest - Bird Food

<http://www.naturechest.com/bifoforinri.html>

Petco – Bird Food; Treats

<http://www.petco.com/shop/en/petcostore/bird/bird-food-and-treats>

Pet Supplies Plus

<http://www.petsuppliesplus.com/thumbnail/Bird/Food-Treats/c/2142/2162.uts>

That Pet Place – Bird Food Supplies

<http://www.thatpetplace.com/bird-supplies/bird-food#!bird-food>

Great Britain Links:

Parrot Essentials UK – Vitamins and Minerals for birds

<http://www.parrotessentials.co.uk/vitamins-minerals/>

Scarletts Parrot Essentials UK – Bird Food

<http://www.scarlettsparrotessentials.co.uk/food>

Seapets – Bird Food

<https://www.seapets.co.uk/bird-supplies/bird-food/bird-seeds>

ZooPlus

<http://www.zooplus.co.uk/shop/birds/bird_food/parrot>

Bird Food UK

<http://www.birdfood.co.uk/ctrl/node:114;page:2;/bird_food s>

Ideal Price UK

<http://www.idealprice.co.uk/compare.html?q=conure%20food>

Northern Parrots – Parrot Treatments

<http://www.northernparrots.com/treatments-and-cures-dept139/>

Index

I

L

M

N

O

Photo Credits

Page 1 Photo by Peter Tan via Wikimedia Commons, <https://commons.wikimedia.org/wiki/File:Aratinga_solstitialis_-Jurong_Bird_Park_-8a.jpg>

Page 7 Photo by Doug Janson via Wikimedia Commons, <https://commons.wikimedia.org/wiki/File:Aratinga_solstitialis-20040821.jpg>

Page 8 Photo by Frank Wouters via Wikimedia Commons, <https://commons.wikimedia.org/wiki/File:Guaruba_guarouba.jpg>

Page 10 Photo by Benny Mazur via Wikimedia Commons, <https://commons.wikimedia.org/wiki/File:Guaruba_guarouba_-National_Aviary_-USA-6-2c.jpg>

Page 14 Photo by Jun Dela Cruz via Wikimedia Commons, <https://commons.wikimedia.org/wiki/File:Aratinga_solstitialis_-four_on_a_perch_in_captivity-8a.jpg>

Page 40 Photo by Daniel Ramirez via Wikimedia Commons, <https://commons.wikimedia.org/wiki/File:Aratinga_solstitialis_-Honolulu_Zoo,_Hawaii,_USA-8a.jpg>

Page 42 Photo by user Kevin via Wikimedia Commons, <https://commons.wikimedia.org/wiki/File:Aratinga_acuticaud ata_-Miami_-Florida_-feral-8a.jpg >

Page 50 Photo by Chris Gin via Wikimedia Commons, <https://commons.wikimedia.org/wiki/File:Sun_Conure.jpg>

Page 54 Photo by user Richard via Wikimedia Commons, <https://commons.wikimedia.org/wiki/File:Blue-crowned_Conure_(Aratinga_acuticaudata)_-back.jpg>

Page 85 Photo by Michael Spencer via Wikimedia Commons, <https://commons.wikimedia.org/wiki/File:Aratinga_solstitialis _-Jurong_Bird_Park-6a.jpg>

Page 94 Photo by user Lionpro2006 via Wikimedia Commons, <https://commons.wikimedia.org/wiki/File:Aratinga_solstitialis _-two_pets-6a.jpg>

Page 110 Photo grabbed from Singing-Wings-Aviary.com <http://www.singing-wings-aviary.com/conures.htm>

Page 113 Photo by Brian Gratwicke via Wikimedia Commons, <https://commons.wikimedia.org/wiki/File:Aratinga_solstitialis _-Hamilton_Zoo_-white_flowers-8.jpg>

Page 120 Photo by user Giannizzzero via Wikimedia Commons, <https://commons.wikimedia.org/wiki/File:Aratinga_Jandaya_-in_tree-8.jpg >

Page 139 Photo by user Kuszapro via Wikimedia Commons, <https://pixabay.com/en/macaw-parrot-bird-pet-wildlife-410144/>

Page 146 Photo by user Robert01 via Wikimedia Commons, <https://commons.wikimedia.org/wiki/File:Guaruba_guarouba_-captive-8a.jpg >

References

"Basic Information Sheet: Conure" Lafeber.com
<http://lafeber.com/vet/basic-information-sheet-for-the-conure/>

"Bringing Pet Birds into UK" Jamescargo.com
<http://www.jamescargo.com/livestock_transport/PetBirdImport.htm>

"Common Conure Diseases" BeautyofBirds.com
<https://www.beautyofbirds.com/conurediseases.html>

"Conures as Pets" Petparrots101.com
<http://petparrots101.com/Conures.asp>

"Conures: Conure Parrot, Conure Types" Animal-World.com
<http://animalworld.com/encyclo/birds/conures/conures.htm>

"Conures: The Little Clowns from the Americas" BeautyofBirds.com
<https://www.beautyofbirds.com/conureinfo.html>

"Golden Parakeet" BirdLife.org

<http://www.birdlife.org/datazone/speciesfactsheet.php?id=9847>

"The Genus Conurus in the West Indies" Jstor.org
<http://www.jstor.org/stable/4070166>

"Types of Conures" Arndt-Verlag.com
<http://www.arndt-verlag.com/conures.htm>

UK Breeders Listings
<http://www.preloved.co.uk/>

"Under Threat – The Green Cheeked Parrot" A-Z.com
< http://a-z-animals.com/blog/under-threat-the-green-cheeked-parrot/>

USA Breeders Listings
<http://www.birdbreeders.com/>

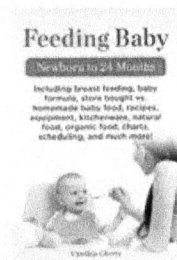

Feeding Baby
Cynthia Cherry
978-1941070000

Axolotl
Lolly Brown
978-0989658430

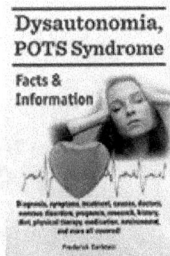

Dysautonomia, POTS
Syndrome
Frederick Earlstein
978-0989658485

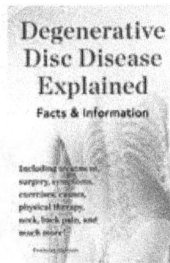

Degenerative Disc
Disease Explained
Frederick Earlstein
978-0989658485

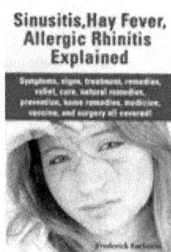

Sinusitis, Hay Fever,
Allergic Rhinitis Explained
Frederick Earlstein
978-1941070024

Wicca
Riley Star
978-1941070130

Zombie Apocalypse
Rex Cutty
978-1941070154

Capybara
Lolly Brown
978-1941070062

Eels As Pets
Lolly Brown
978-1941070167

Scabies and Lice Explained
Frederick Earlstein
978-1941070017

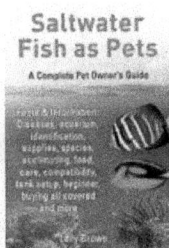

Saltwater Fish As Pets
Lolly Brown
978-0989658461

Torticollis Explained
Frederick Earlstein
978-1941070055

Kennel Cough
Lolly Brown
978-0989658409

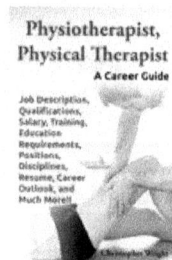

Physiotherapist, Physical
Therapist
Christopher Wright
978-0989658492

Rats, Mice, and Dormice
As Pets
Lolly Brown
978-1941070079

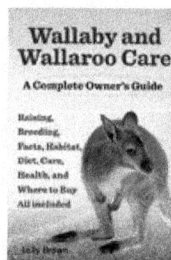

Wallaby and Wallaroo Care
Lolly Brown
978-1941070031

Bodybuilding Supplements
Explained
Jon Shelton
978-1941070239

Demonology
Riley Star
978-19401070314

Pigeon Racing
Lolly Brown
978-1941070307

Dwarf Hamster
Lolly Brown
978-1941070390

Cryptozoology
Rex Cutty
978-1941070406

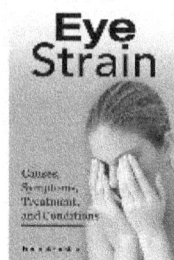

Eye Strain
Frederick Earlstein
978-1941070369

Inez The Miniature Elephant
Asher Ray
978-1941070353

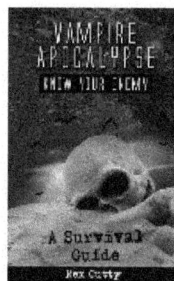

Vampire Apocalypse
Rex Cutty
978-1941070321